The FACTS in the CASE of the DEPARTURE of MISS FINCH

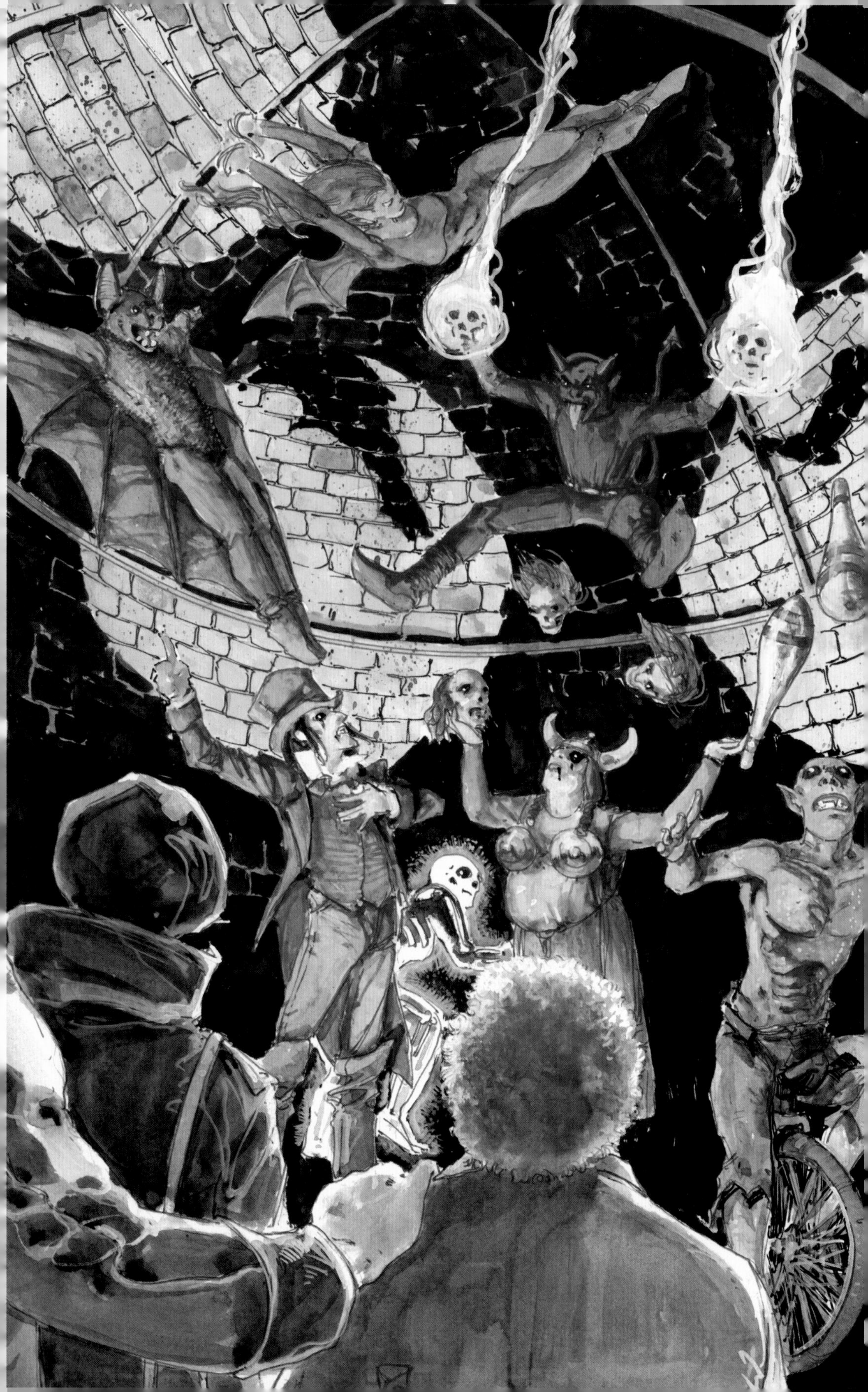

The FACTS in the CASE of the DEPARTURE of MISS FINCH ™

story
Neil Gaiman

art
Michael Zulli

script adaptation & lettering
Todd Klein

Dark Horse Books

executive vice president Neil Hankerson *chief financial officer* Tom Weddle *vice president of publishing* Randy Stradley *vice president of book trade sales* Michael Martens *vice president of marketing* Matt Parkinson *vice president of product development* David Scroggy *vice president of information technology* Dale LaFountain *vice president of production and scheduling* Cara Niece *general counsel* Ken Lizzi *editorial director* Davey Estrada *editor in chief* Dave Marshall *executive senior editor* Scott Allie *senior books editor* Chris Warner *director of print and development* Cary Grazzini *art director* Lia Ribacchi *director of digital publishing* Mark Bernardi

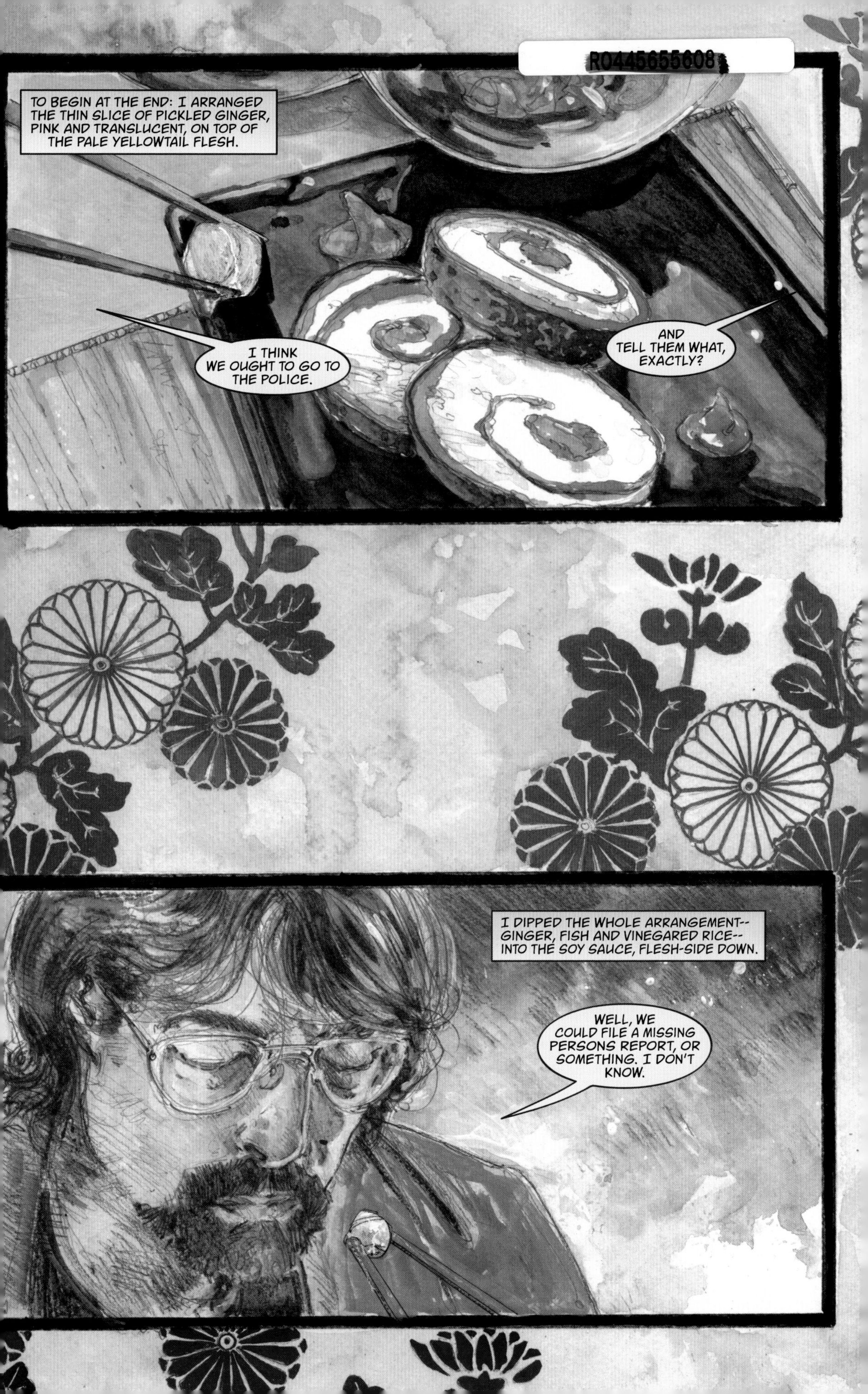
TO BEGIN AT THE END: I ARRANGED THE THIN SLICE OF PICKLED GINGER, PINK AND TRANSLUCENT, ON TOP OF THE PALE YELLOWTAIL FLESH.
I THINK WE OUGHT TO GO TO THE POLICE.
AND TELL THEM WHAT, EXACTLY?
I DIPPED THE WHOLE ARRANGEMENT--GINGER, FISH AND VINEGARED RICE--INTO THE SOY SAUCE, FLESH-SIDE DOWN.
WELL, WE COULD FILE A MISSING PERSONS REPORT, OR SOMETHING. I DON'T KNOW.

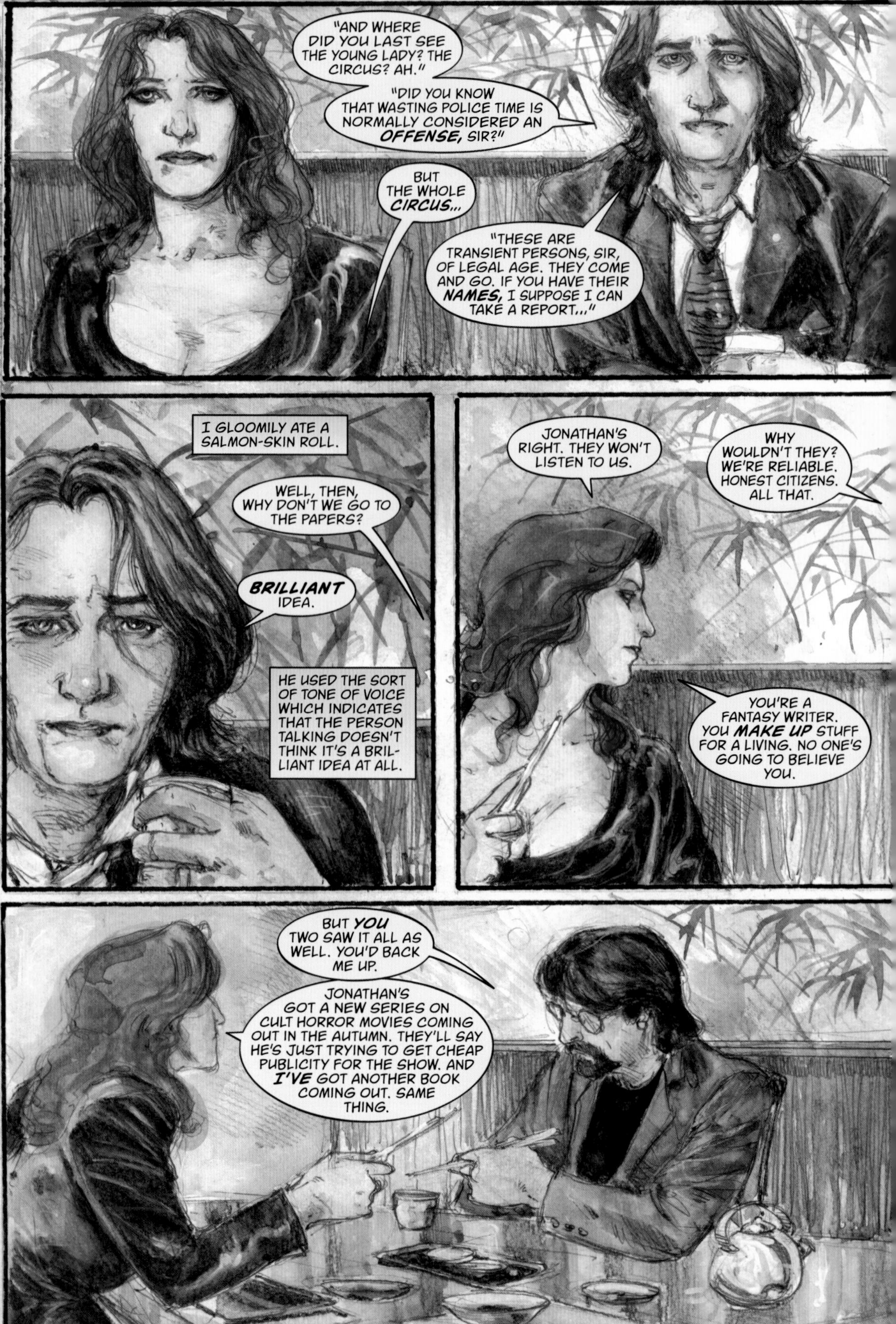
"AND WHERE DID YOU LAST SEE THE YOUNG LADY? THE CIRCUS? AH."
"DID YOU KNOW THAT WASTING POLICE TIME IS NORMALLY CONSIDERED AN OFFENSE, SIR?"
BUT THE WHOLE CIRCUS...
"THESE ARE TRANSIENT PERSONS, SIR, OF LEGAL AGE. THEY COME AND GO. IF YOU HAVE THEIR NAMES, I SUPPOSE I CAN TAKE A REPORT..."
I GLOOMILY ATE A SALMON-SKIN ROLL.
WELL, THEN, WHY DON'T WE GO TO THE PAPERS?
BRILLIANT IDEA.
HE USED THE SORT OF TONE OF VOICE WHICH INDICATES THAT THE PERSON TALKING DOESN'T THINK IT'S A BRILLIANT IDEA AT ALL.
JONATHAN'S RIGHT. THEY WON'T LISTEN TO US.
WHY WOULDN'T THEY? WE'RE RELIABLE. HONEST CITIZENS. ALL THAT.
YOU'RE A FANTASY WRITER. YOU MAKE UP STUFF FOR A LIVING. NO ONE'S GOING TO BELIEVE YOU.
BUT YOU TWO SAW IT ALL AS WELL. YOU'D BACK ME UP.
JONATHAN'S GOT A NEW SERIES ON CULT HORROR MOVIES COMING OUT IN THE AUTUMN. THEY'LL SAY HE'S JUST TRYING TO GET CHEAP PUBLICITY FOR THE SHOW. AND I'VE GOT ANOTHER BOOK COMING OUT. SAME THING.

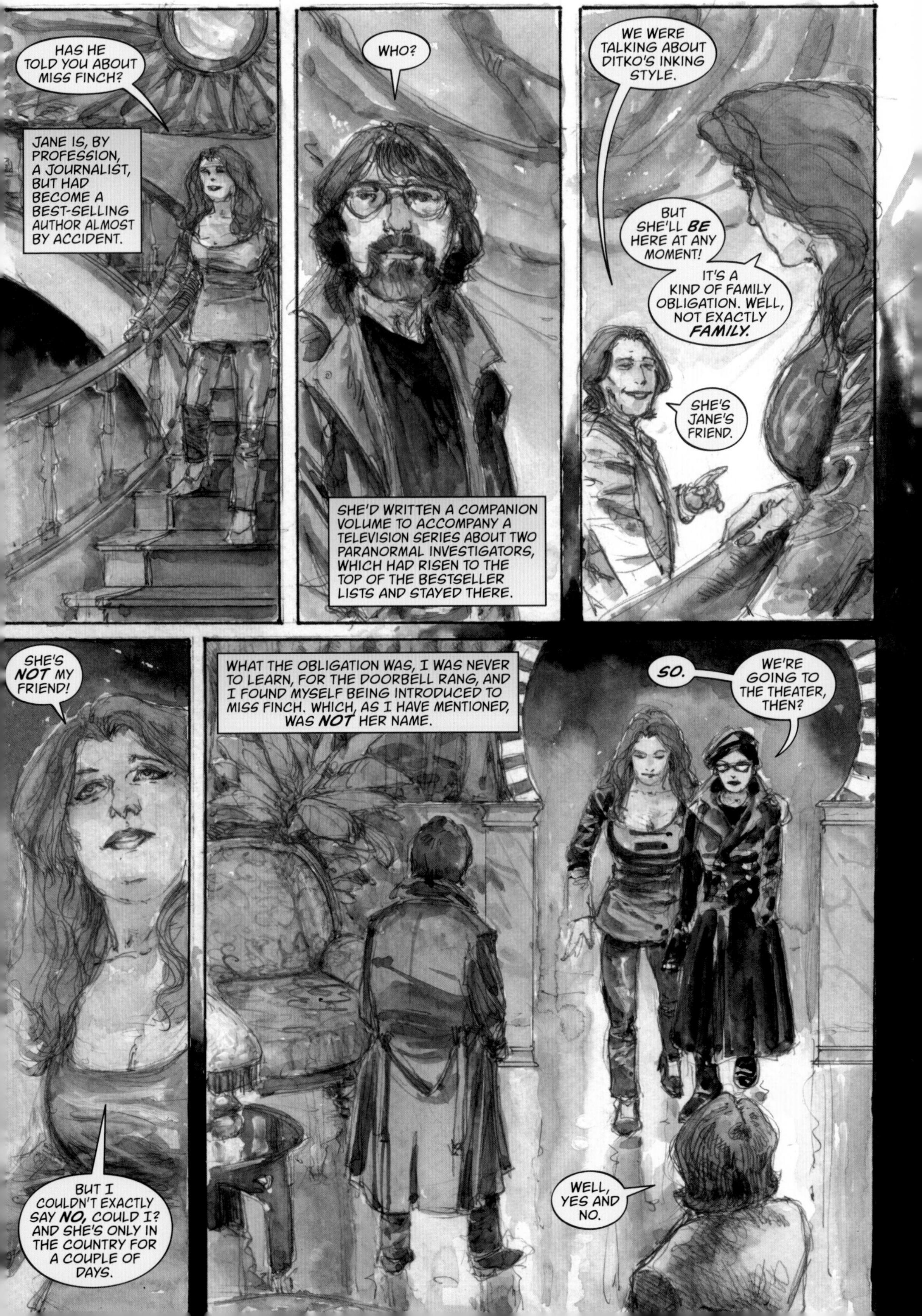
HAS HE TOLD YOU ABOUT MISS FINCH?
JANE IS, BY PROFESSION, A JOURNALIST, BUT HAD BECOME A BEST-SELLING AUTHOR ALMOST BY ACCIDENT.
WHO?
SHE'D WRITTEN A COMPANION VOLUME TO ACCOMPANY A TELEVISION SERIES ABOUT TWO PARANORMAL INVESTIGATORS, WHICH HAD RISEN TO THE TOP OF THE BESTSELLER LISTS AND STAYED THERE.
WE WERE TALKING ABOUT DITKO'S INKING STYLE.
BUT SHE'LL **BE** HERE AT ANY MOMENT!
IT'S A KIND OF FAMILY OBLIGATION. WELL, NOT EXACTLY ***FAMILY.***
SHE'S JANE'S FRIEND.
SHE'S **NOT** MY FRIEND!
BUT I COULDN'T EXACTLY SAY **NO,** COULD I? AND SHE'S ONLY IN THE COUNTRY FOR A COUPLE OF DAYS.
WHAT THE OBLIGATION WAS, I WAS NEVER TO LEARN, FOR THE DOORBELL RANG, AND I FOUND MYSELF BEING INTRODUCED TO MISS FINCH. WHICH, AS I HAVE MENTIONED, WAS **NOT** HER NAME.
SO.
WE'RE GOING TO THE THEATER, THEN?
WELL, YES AND NO.

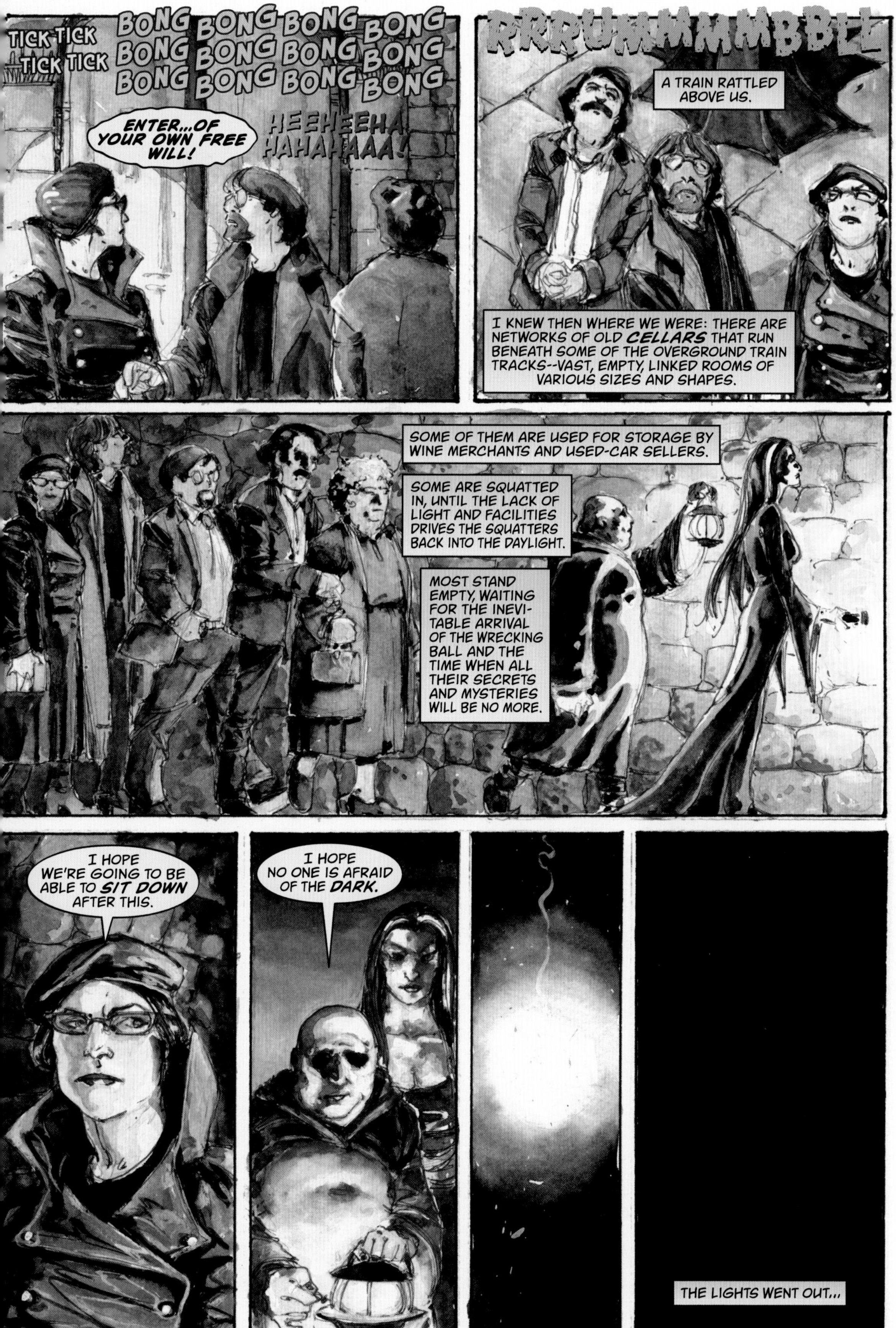
TICK TICK TICK TICK
BONG BONG BONG BONG BONG BONG BONG BONG BONG BONG BONG BONG BONG
ENTER...OF YOUR OWN FREE WILL!
HEEHEEHA HAHAHAAA!
RRRUMMMMMBBLE
A TRAIN RATTLED ABOVE US.
I KNEW THEN WHERE WE WERE: THERE ARE NETWORKS OF OLD CELLARS THAT RUN BENEATH SOME OF THE OVERGROUND TRAIN TRACKS--VAST, EMPTY, LINKED ROOMS OF VARIOUS SIZES AND SHAPES.
SOME OF THEM ARE USED FOR STORAGE BY WINE MERCHANTS AND USED-CAR SELLERS.
SOME ARE SQUATTED IN, UNTIL THE LACK OF LIGHT AND FACILITIES DRIVES THE SQUATTERS BACK INTO THE DAYLIGHT.
MOST STAND EMPTY, WAITING FOR THE INEVI-TABLE ARRIVAL OF THE WRECKING BALL AND THE TIME WHEN ALL THEIR SECRETS AND MYSTERIES WILL BE NO MORE.
I HOPE WE'RE GOING TO BE ABLE TO SIT DOWN AFTER THIS.
I HOPE NO ONE IS AFRAID OF THE DARK.
THE LIGHTS WENT OUT...

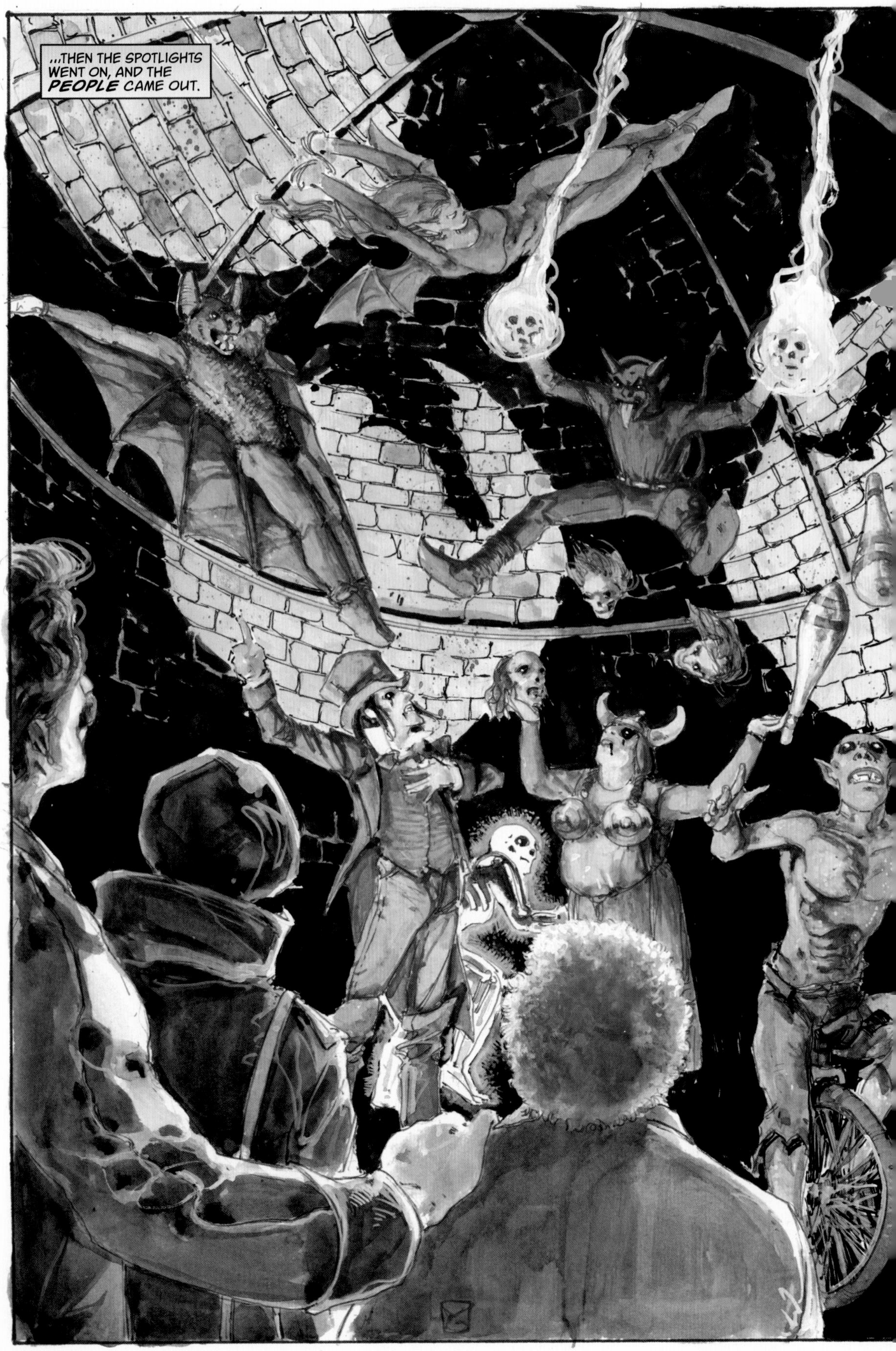
...THEN THE SPOTLIGHTS WENT ON, AND THE *PEOPLE* CAME OUT.

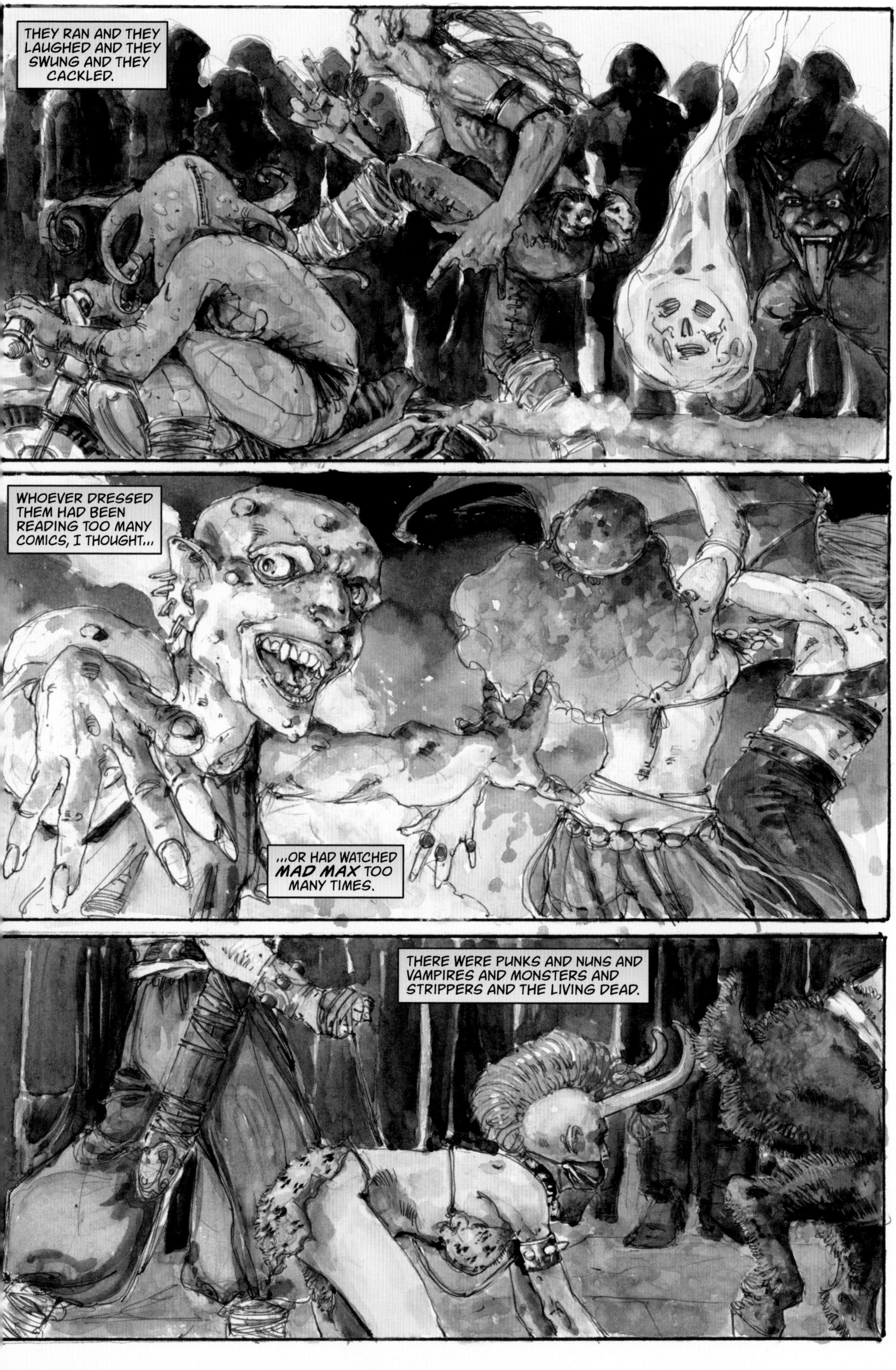
THEY RAN AND THEY LAUGHED AND THEY SWUNG AND THEY CACKLED.
WHOEVER DRESSED THEM HAD BEEN READING TOO MANY COMICS, I THOUGHT...
...OR HAD WATCHED MAD MAX TOO MANY TIMES.
THERE WERE PUNKS AND NUNS AND VAMPIRES AND MONSTERS AND STRIPPERS AND THE LIVING DEAD.

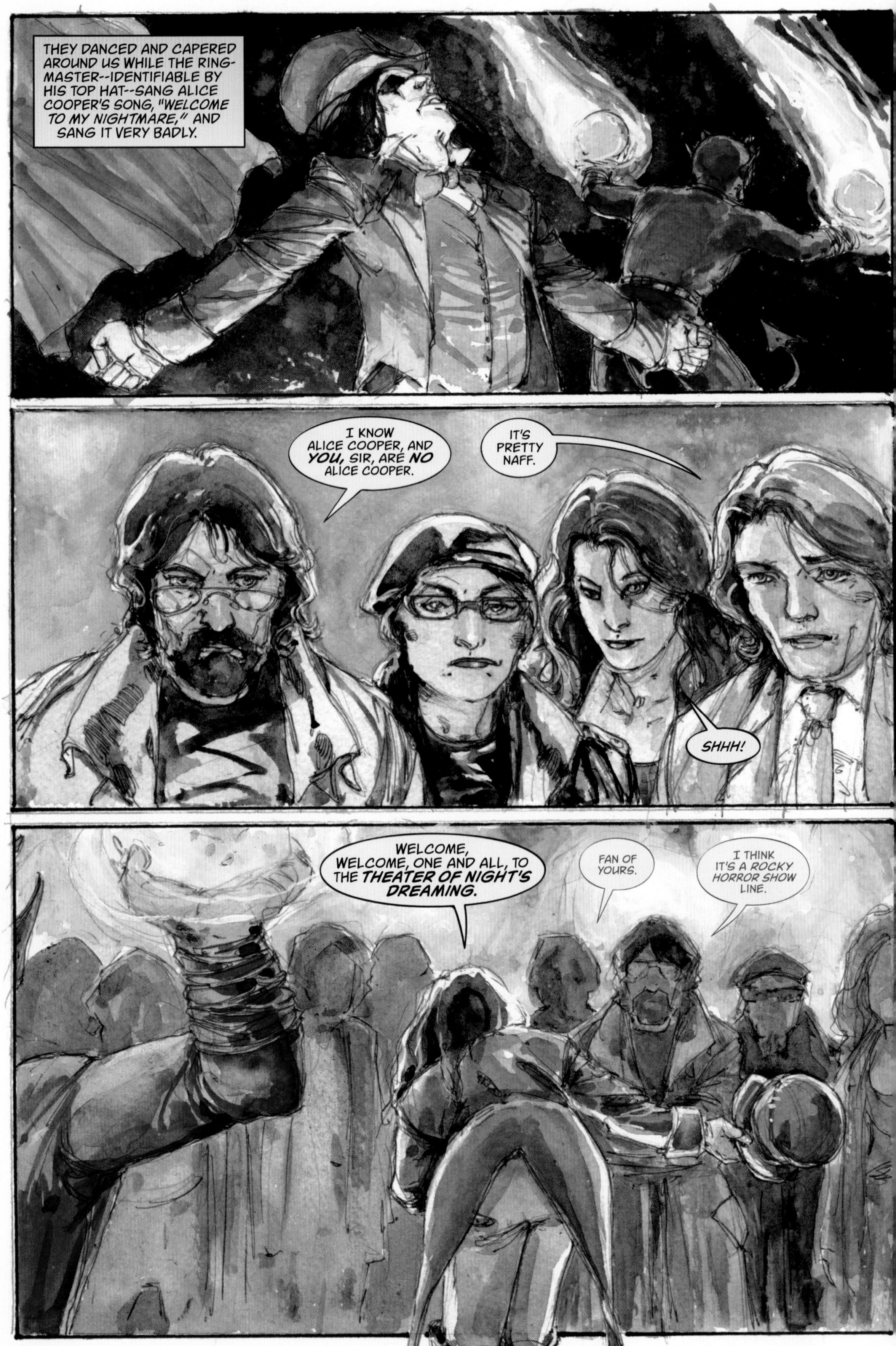
THEY DANCED AND CAPERED AROUND US WHILE THE RING-MASTER--IDENTIFIABLE BY HIS TOP HAT--SANG ALICE COOPER'S SONG, "WELCOME TO MY NIGHTMARE," AND SANG IT VERY BADLY.
I KNOW ALICE COOPER, AND YOU, SIR, ARE NO ALICE COOPER.
IT'S PRETTY NAFF.
SHHH!
WELCOME, WELCOME, ONE AND ALL, TO THE THEATER OF NIGHT'S DREAMING.
FAN OF YOURS.
I THINK IT'S A ROCKY HORROR SHOW LINE.

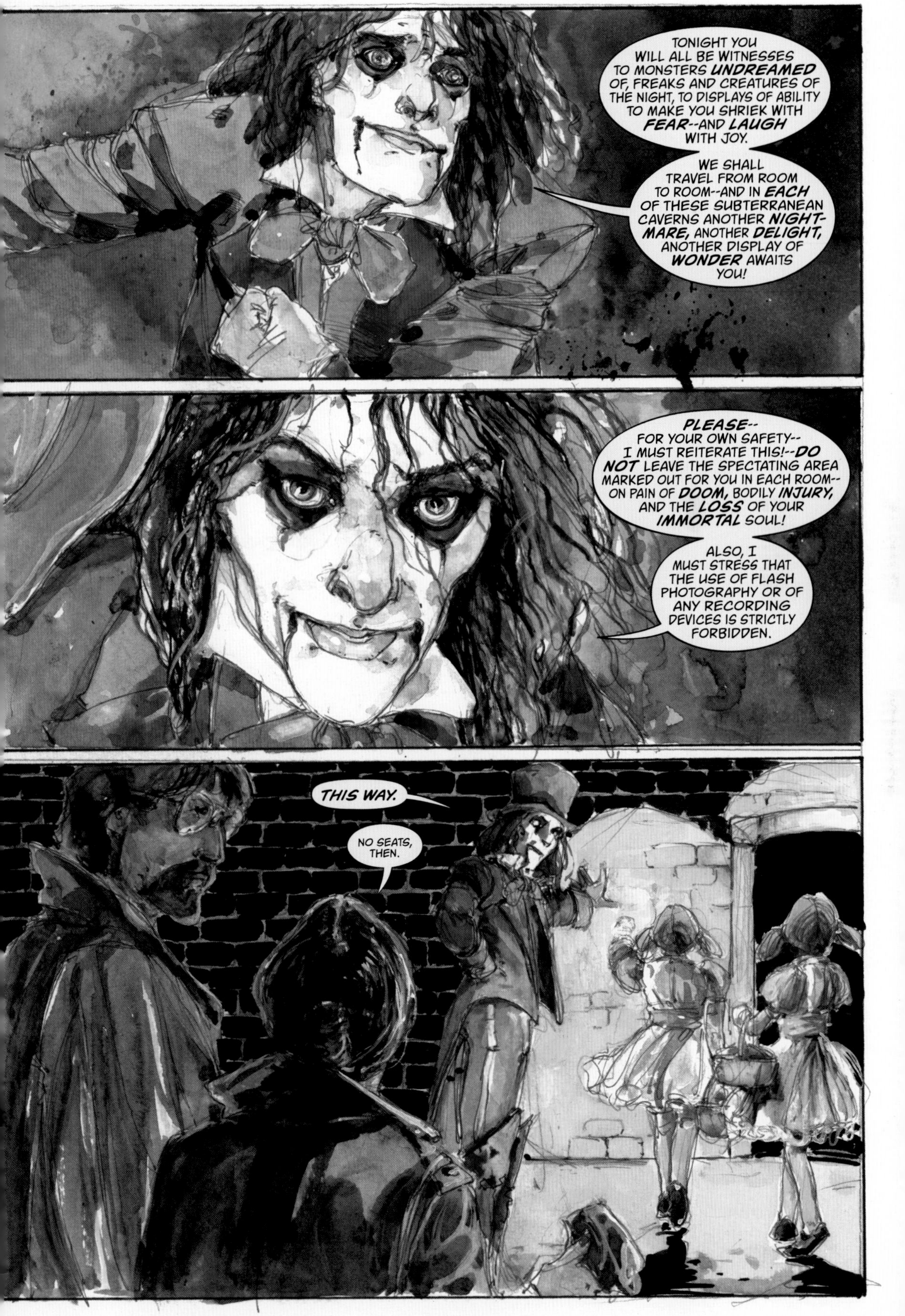
TONIGHT YOU WILL ALL BE WITNESSES TO MONSTERS UNDREAMED OF, FREAKS AND CREATURES OF THE NIGHT, TO DISPLAYS OF ABILITY TO MAKE YOU SHRIEK WITH FEAR--AND LAUGH WITH JOY.
WE SHALL TRAVEL FROM ROOM TO ROOM--AND IN EACH OF THESE SUBTERRANEAN CAVERNS ANOTHER NIGHT-MARE, ANOTHER DELIGHT, ANOTHER DISPLAY OF WONDER AWAITS YOU!
PLEASE-- FOR YOUR OWN SAFETY-- I MUST REITERATE THIS!--DO NOT LEAVE THE SPECTATING AREA MARKED OUT FOR YOU IN EACH ROOM--ON PAIN OF DOOM, BODILY INJURY, AND THE LOSS OF YOUR IMMORTAL SOUL!
ALSO, I MUST STRESS THAT THE USE OF FLASH PHOTOGRAPHY OR OF ANY RECORDING DEVICES IS STRICTLY FORBIDDEN.
THIS WAY.
NO SEATS, THEN.

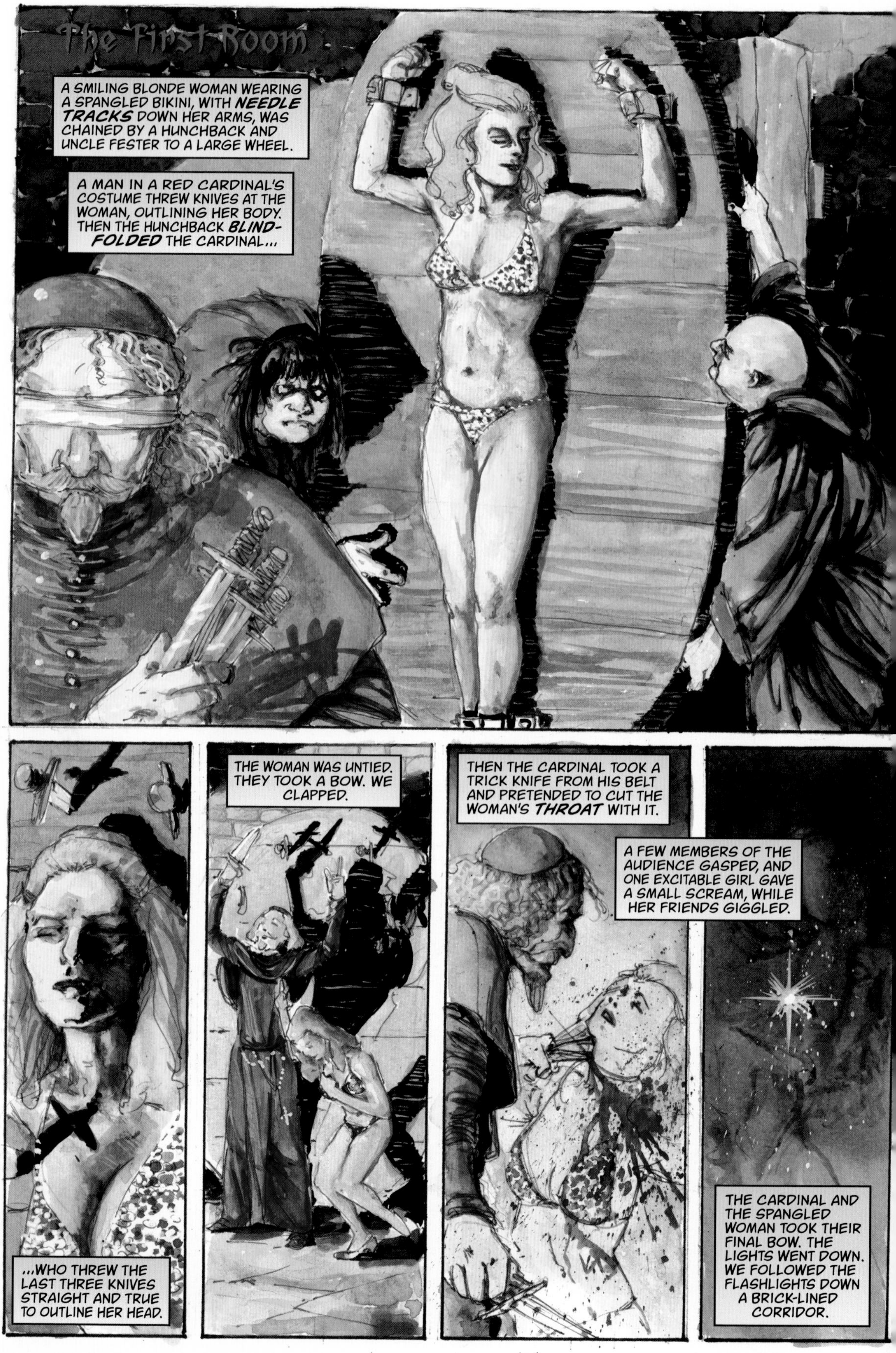
The First Room
A SMILING BLONDE WOMAN WEARING A SPANGLED BIKINI, WITH NEEDLE TRACKS DOWN HER ARMS, WAS CHAINED BY A HUNCHBACK AND UNCLE FESTER TO A LARGE WHEEL.
A MAN IN A RED CARDINAL'S COSTUME THREW KNIVES AT THE WOMAN, OUTLINING HER BODY. THEN THE HUNCHBACK BLIND-FOLDED THE CARDINAL...
...WHO THREW THE LAST THREE KNIVES STRAIGHT AND TRUE TO OUTLINE HER HEAD.
THE WOMAN WAS UNTIED. THEY TOOK A BOW. WE CLAPPED.
THEN THE CARDINAL TOOK A TRICK KNIFE FROM HIS BELT AND PRETENDED TO CUT THE WOMAN'S THROAT WITH IT.
A FEW MEMBERS OF THE AUDIENCE GASPED, AND ONE EXCITABLE GIRL GAVE A SMALL SCREAM, WHILE HER FRIENDS GIGGLED.
THE CARDINAL AND THE SPANGLED WOMAN TOOK THEIR FINAL BOW. THE LIGHTS WENT DOWN. WE FOLLOWED THE FLASHLIGHTS DOWN A BRICK-LINED CORRIDOR.

THE SMELL OF DAMP WAS WORSE IN HERE; IT SMELLED MUSTY AND FORGOTTEN. I COULD HEAR SOMEWHERE THE DRIP OF RAIN. THE RINGMASTER INTRODUCED *THE CREATURE.*

...STITCHED TOGETHER IN THE LABORATORIES OF THE NIGHT, THE CREATURE IS CAPABLE OF *ASTONISHING* FEATS OF STRENGTH!

...AND HE HELD BACK A DUNE BUGGY (DRIVEN BY THE VAMPIRE WOMAN) AT *FULL THROTTLE.*

THE *MAKE-UP* WAS LESS THAN CONVINCING, BUT THE CREATURE LIFTED A STONE BLOCK WITH FAT UNCLE FESTER SITTING ON IT....

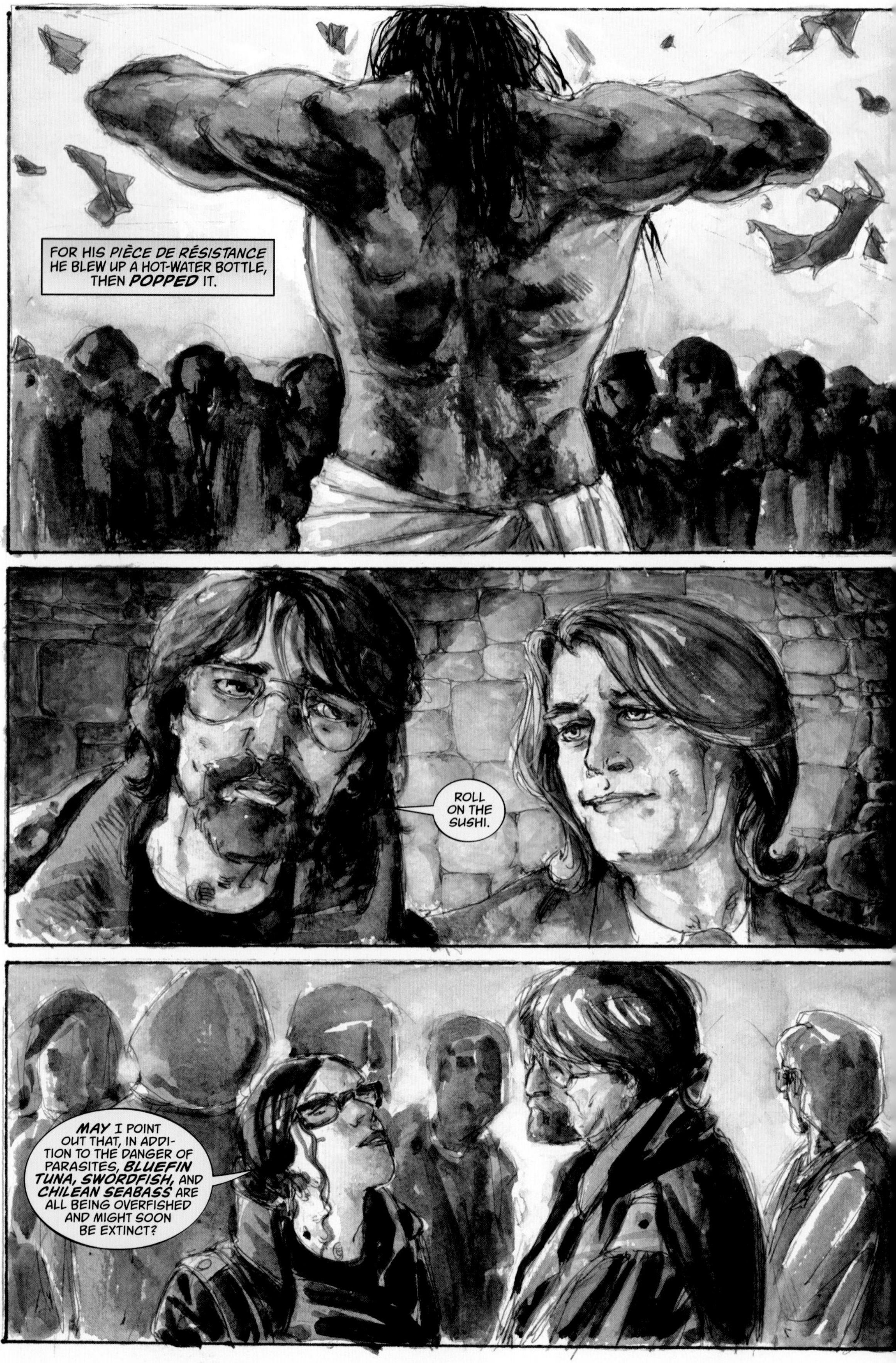
FOR HIS *PIÈCE DE RÉSISTANCE* HE BLEW UP A HOT-WATER BOTTLE, THEN ***POPPED*** IT.
ROLL ON THE SUSHI.
MAY I POINT OUT THAT, IN ADDITION TO THE DANGER OF PARASITES, ***BLUEFIN TUNA, SWORDFISH,*** AND ***CHILEAN SEABASS*** ARE ALL BEING OVERFISHED AND MIGHT SOON BE EXTINCT?

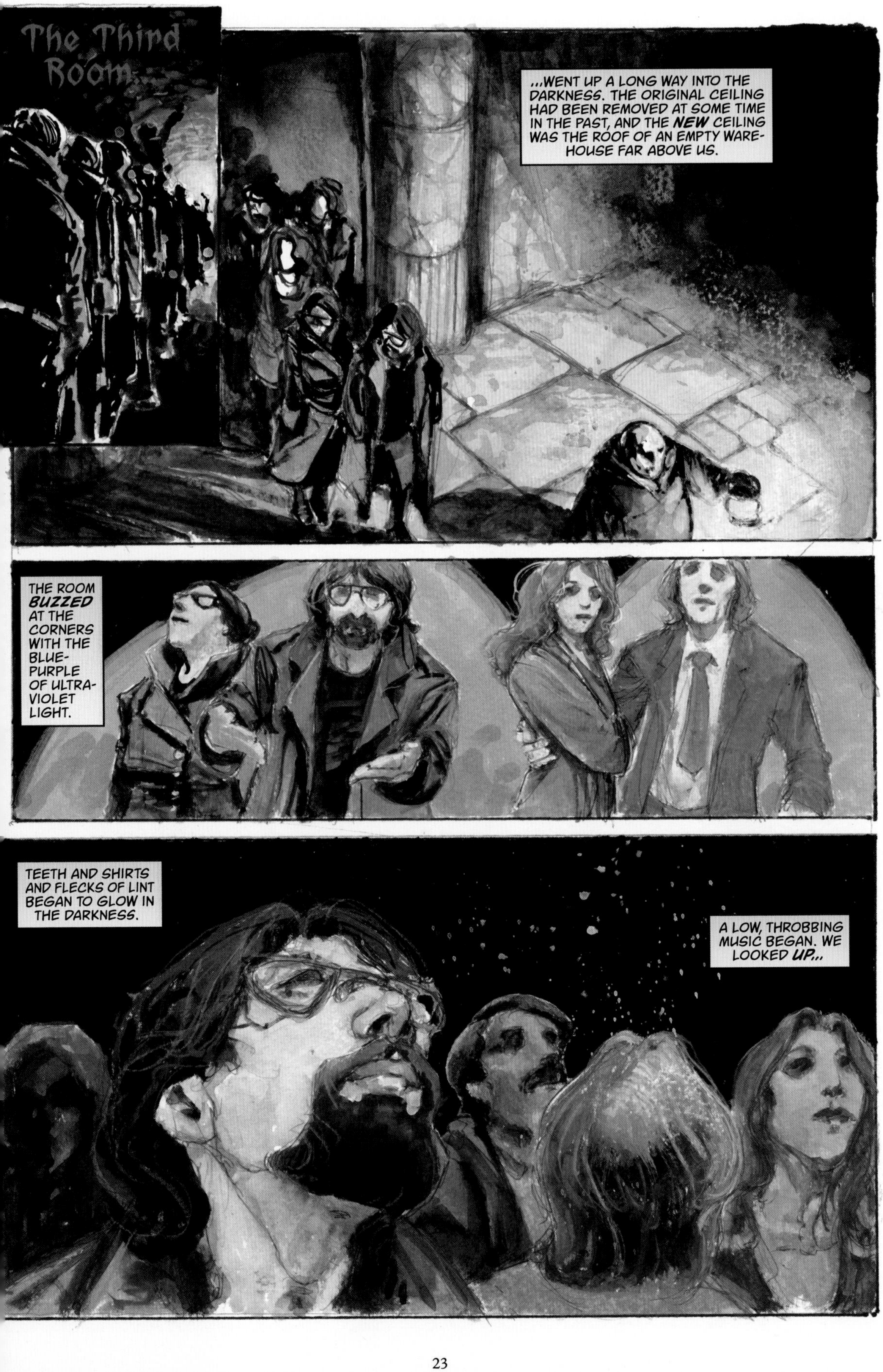
The Third Room...
...WENT UP A LONG WAY INTO THE DARKNESS. THE ORIGINAL CEILING HAD BEEN REMOVED AT SOME TIME IN THE PAST, AND THE NEW CEILING WAS THE ROOF OF AN EMPTY WARE-HOUSE FAR ABOVE US.
THE ROOM BUZZED AT THE CORNERS WITH THE BLUE-PURPLE OF ULTRA-VIOLET LIGHT.
TEETH AND SHIRTS AND FLECKS OF LINT BEGAN TO GLOW IN THE DARKNESS.
A LOW, THROBBING MUSIC BEGAN. WE LOOKED UP...

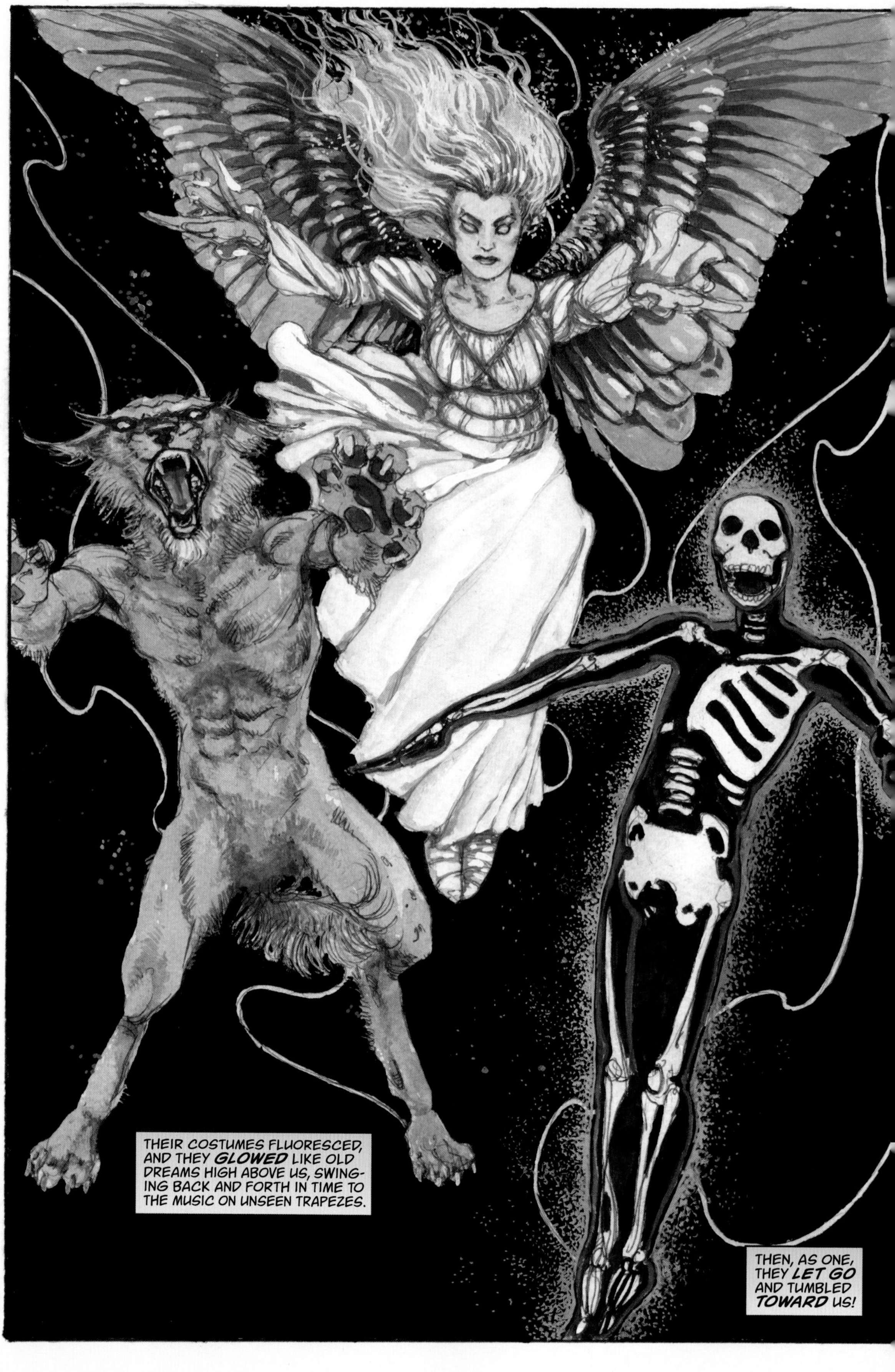
THEIR COSTUMES FLUORESCED, AND THEY GLOWED LIKE OLD DREAMS HIGH ABOVE US, SWING-ING BACK AND FORTH IN TIME TO THE MUSIC ON UNSEEN TRAPEZES.
THEN, AS ONE, THEY LET GO AND TUMBLED TOWARD US!

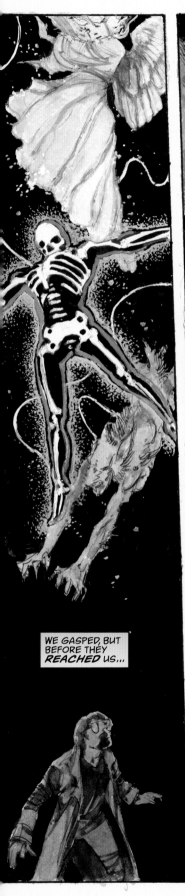

...THEY BOUNCED ON THE AIR AND *ROSE UP* AGAIN, LIKE YO-YOS, AND CLIMBED BACK ON THEIR TRAPEZES, ATTACHED TO THE ROOF BY RUBBER CORDS.

WE GASPED, BUT BEFORE THEY *REACHED* US...

THEY BOUNCED AND DOVE AND *SWAM* THROUGH THE AIR ABOVE US WHILE WE CLAPPED AND GASPED AND WATCHED THEM IN HAPPY SILENCE.

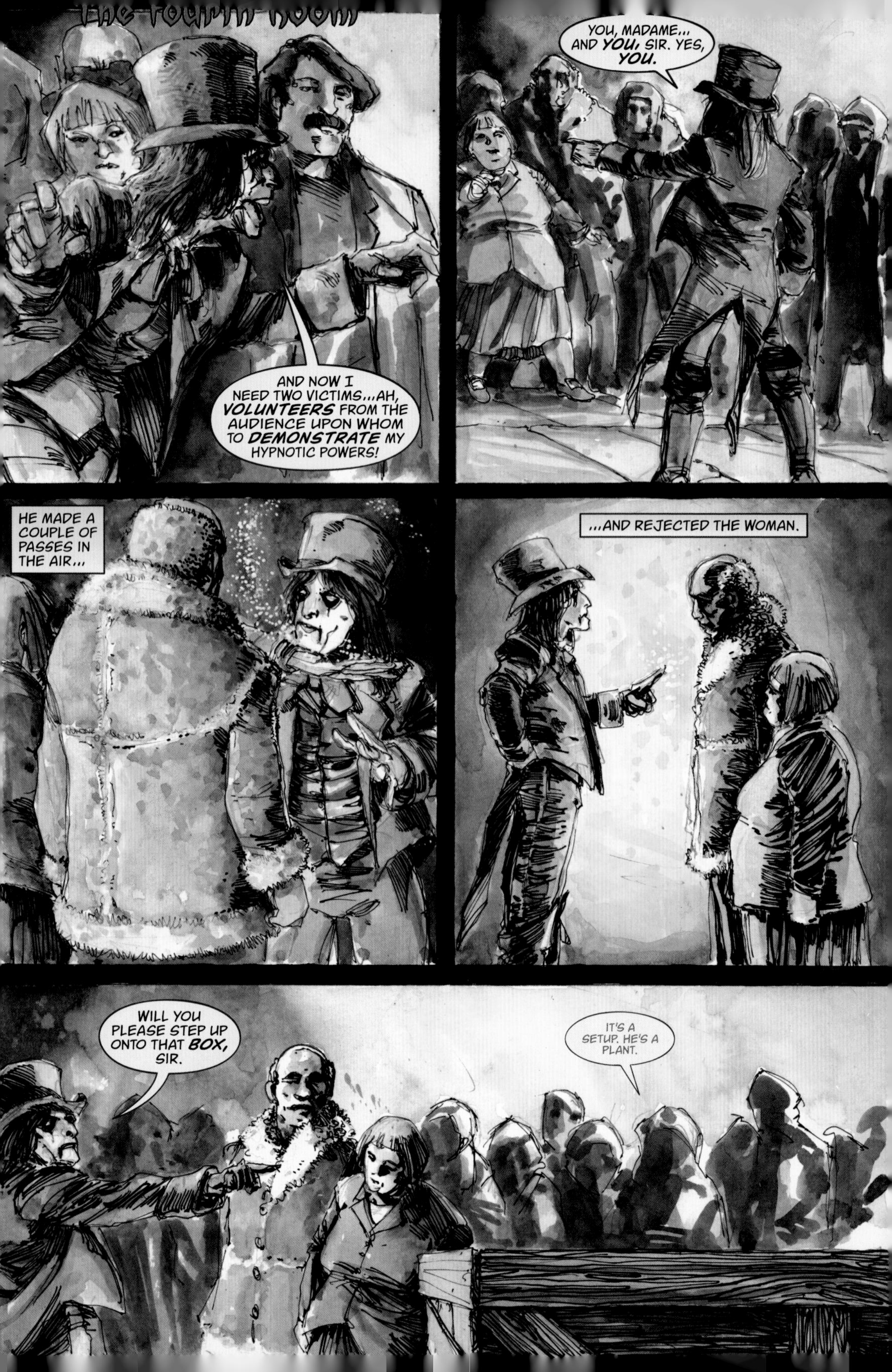
AND NOW I NEED TWO VICTIMS...AH, VOLUNTEERS FROM THE AUDIENCE UPON WHOM TO DEMONSTRATE MY HYPNOTIC POWERS!
YOU, MADAME... AND YOU, SIR. YES, YOU.
HE MADE A COUPLE OF PASSES IN THE AIR...
...AND REJECTED THE WOMAN.
WILL YOU PLEASE STEP UP ONTO THAT BOX, SIR.
IT'S A SETUP. HE'S A PLANT.

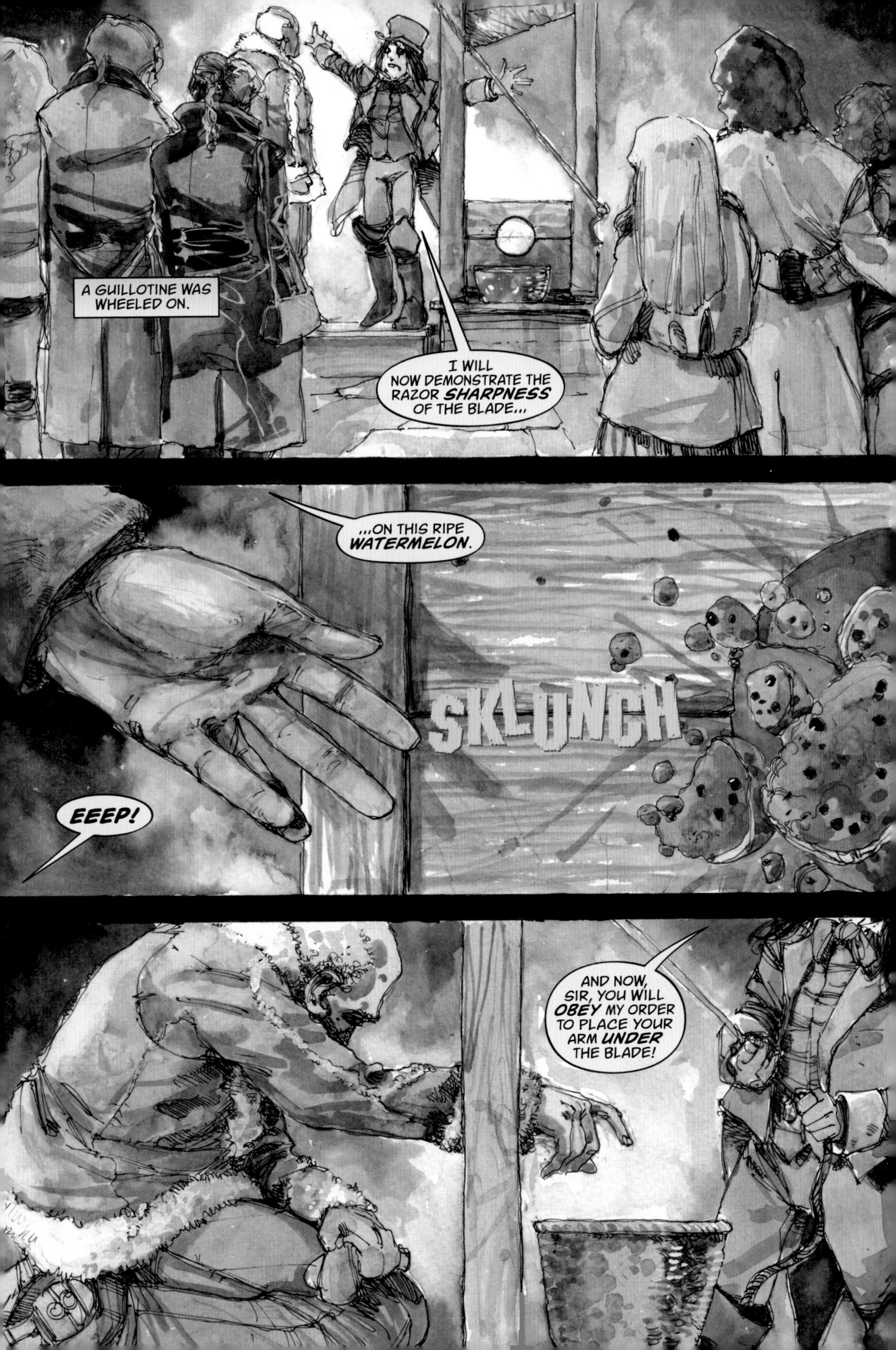
A GUILLOTINE WAS WHEELED ON.
I WILL NOW DEMONSTRATE THE RAZOR SHARPNESS OF THE BLADE...
...ON THIS RIPE WATERMELON.
SKLUNCH
EEEP!
AND NOW, SIR, YOU WILL OBEY MY ORDER TO PLACE YOUR ARM UNDER THE BLADE!

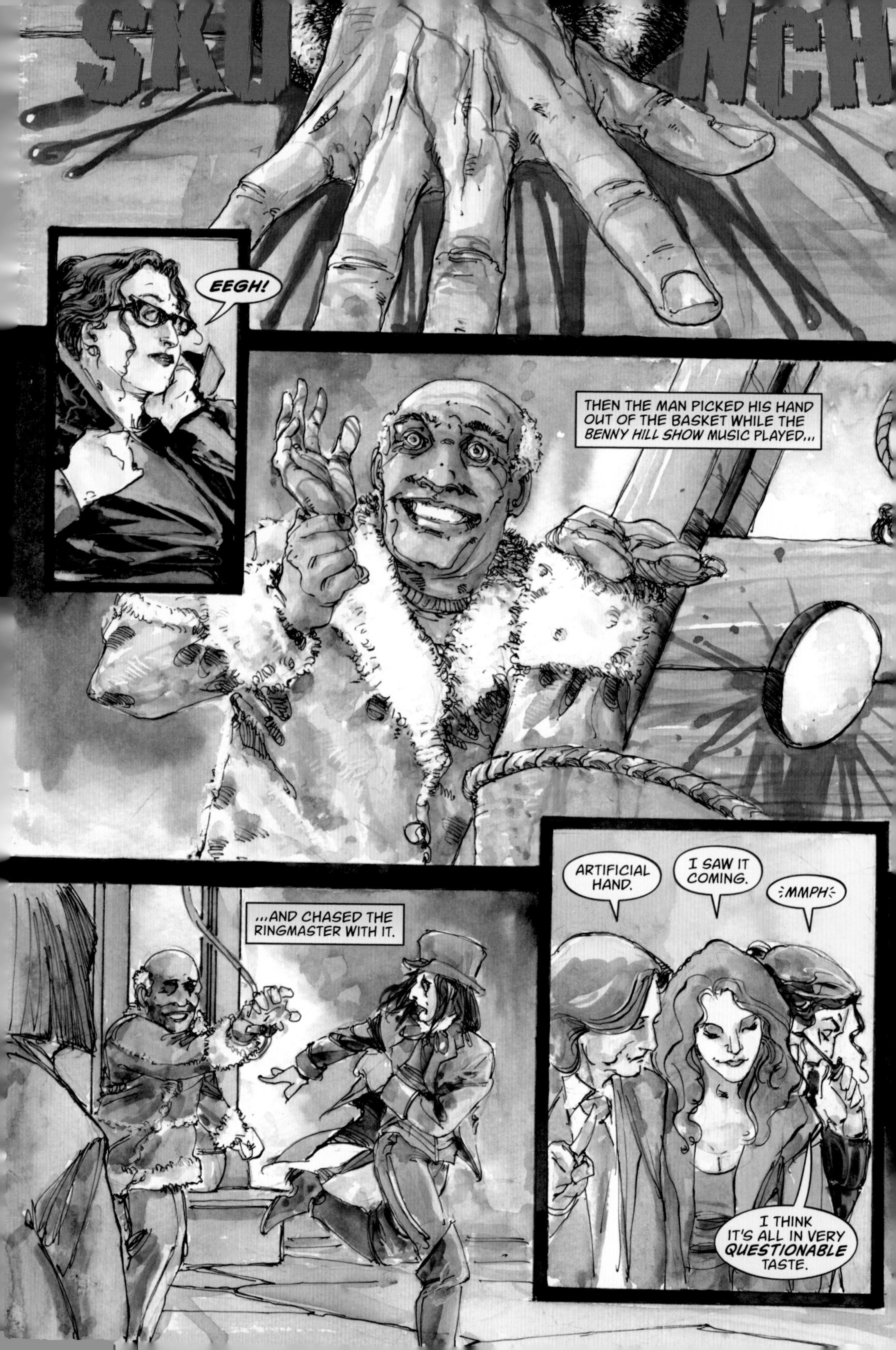
SKU NCH
EEGH!
THEN THE MAN PICKED HIS HAND OUT OF THE BASKET WHILE THE BENNY HILL SHOW MUSIC PLAYED...
...AND CHASED THE RINGMASTER WITH IT.
ARTIFICIAL HAND.
I SAW IT COMING.
MMPH
I THINK IT'S ALL IN VERY QUESTIONABLE TASTE.

The Fifth Room

ALL THE LIGHTS WENT ON. A YOUNG MAN WAS SELLING BEER AND ORANGE JUICE AND BOTTLES OF WATER.

JONATHAN WENT TO USE THE TOILETS...

...WHILE JANE WENT TO GET THE DRINKS.

WHICH LEFT ME TO MAKE AWKWARD CONVERSATION WITH MISS FINCH.

SO, I UNDERSTAND YOU'VE NOT BEEN BACK IN ENGLAND LONG.

I'VE BEEN IN *KOMODO* STUDYING THE DRAGONS. DO YOU KNOW WHY THEY GREW SO BIG?

ER...

THEY ADAPTED TO PREY UPON THE PYGMY ELEPHANTS.

THERE WERE *PYGMY* ELEPHANTS?

OH, YES. IT'S BASIC ISLAND BIOGEOLOGY--ANIMALS WILL NATURALLY TEND TOWARD EITHER GIGANTISM OR PYGMYISM.

THERE ARE *EQUATIONS*, YOU SEE...

THIS WAS *MUCH* MORE FUN THAN BEING LECTURED ON SUSHI FLUKES. AS MISS FINCH TALKED HER FACE BECAME MORE ANIMATED, AND I FOUND MYSELF WARMING TO HER AS SHE EXPLAINED WHY AND HOW SOME ANIMALS GREW WHILE OTHERS SHRANK.

JANE HAD OUR DRINKS.

TELL ME... I'VE BEEN READING A LOT OF CRYPTO-ZOOLOGICAL JOURNALS FOR THE NEXT *GUIDES TO THE UNEXPLAINED* I'M DOING. AS A BIOLOGIST--

BIO-*GEOLO*-GIST.

The Sixth Room

PRESENTING...THE *PAINMAKER!*

THE SPOTLIGHT SWUNG TO AN ABNORMALLY THIN YOUNG MAN HANGING FROM *HOOKS* THROUGH HIS NIPPLES. THE TWO GIRLS HELPED HIM TO THE GROUND AND HANDED HIM HIS PROPS.

WASN'T HE ON THE SHOW, YEARS AGO?

HE LIFTED WEIGHTS WITH A *PIERCING* THROUGH HIS TONGUE,...

...PUT SEVERAL FERRETS INTO HIS BATHING TRUNKS,...

YEAH. REALLY NICE GUY. HE LIT A FIREWORK HELD IN HIS *TEETH.*

...AND, FOR HIS FINAL TRICK, ALLOWED THE TALLER GIRL TO USE HIS STOMACH AS A *DARTBOARD* FOR ACCURATELY THROWN HYPODERMIC NEEDLES.

I THOUGHT YOU SAID THERE WERE NO *ANIMALS.*

HOW DO YOU THINK THOSE POOR FERRETS FEEL ABOUT BEING STUFFED INTO THAT YOUNG MAN'S NETHER REGIONS?

I SUPPOSE IT DEPENDS MOSTLY ON WHETHER THEY'RE *BOY* FERRETS OR *GIRL* FERRETS.

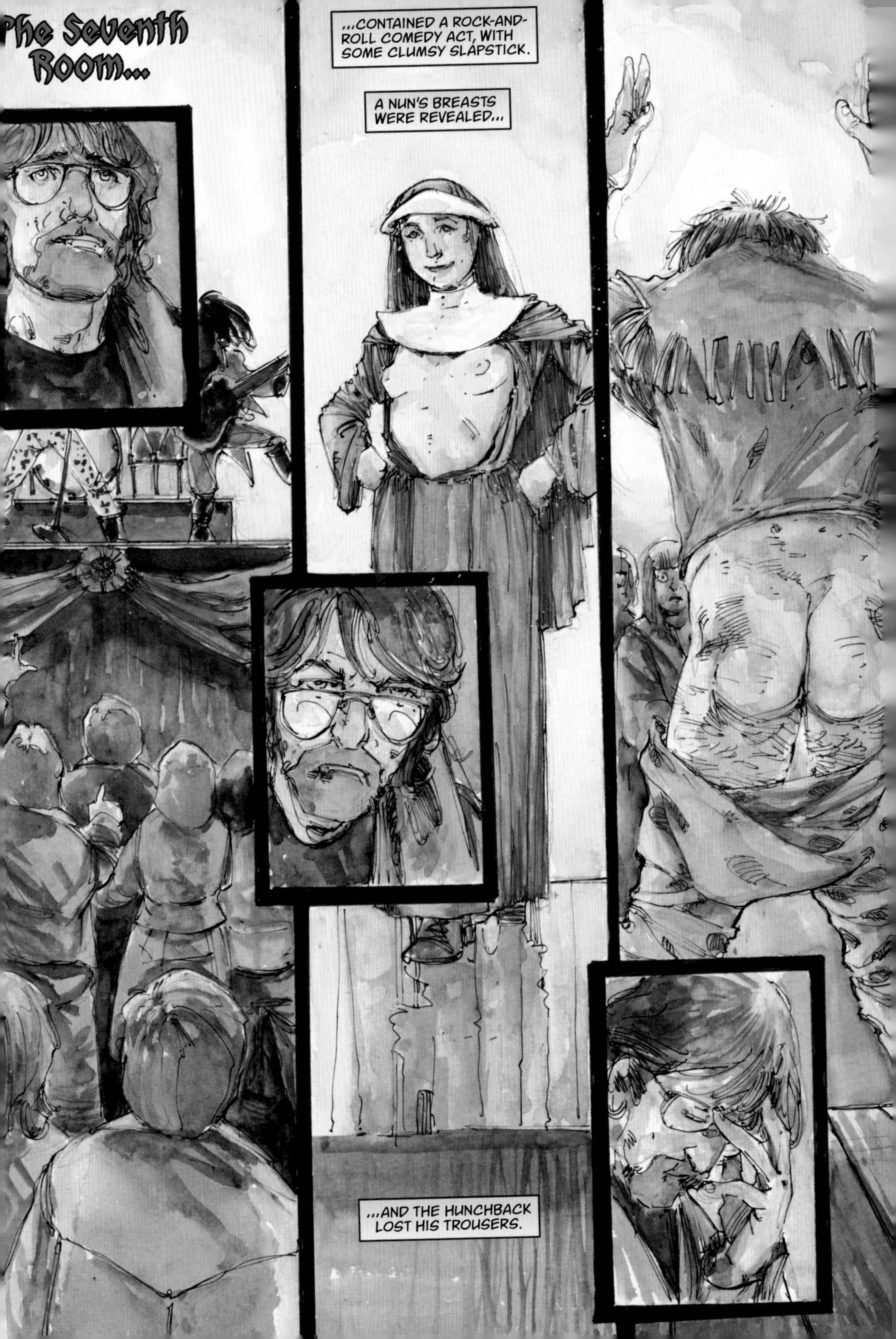
The Seventh Room...
...CONTAINED A ROCK-AND-ROLL COMEDY ACT, WITH SOME CLUMSY SLAPSTICK.
A NUN'S BREASTS WERE REVEALED...
...AND THE HUNCHBACK LOST HIS TROUSERS.

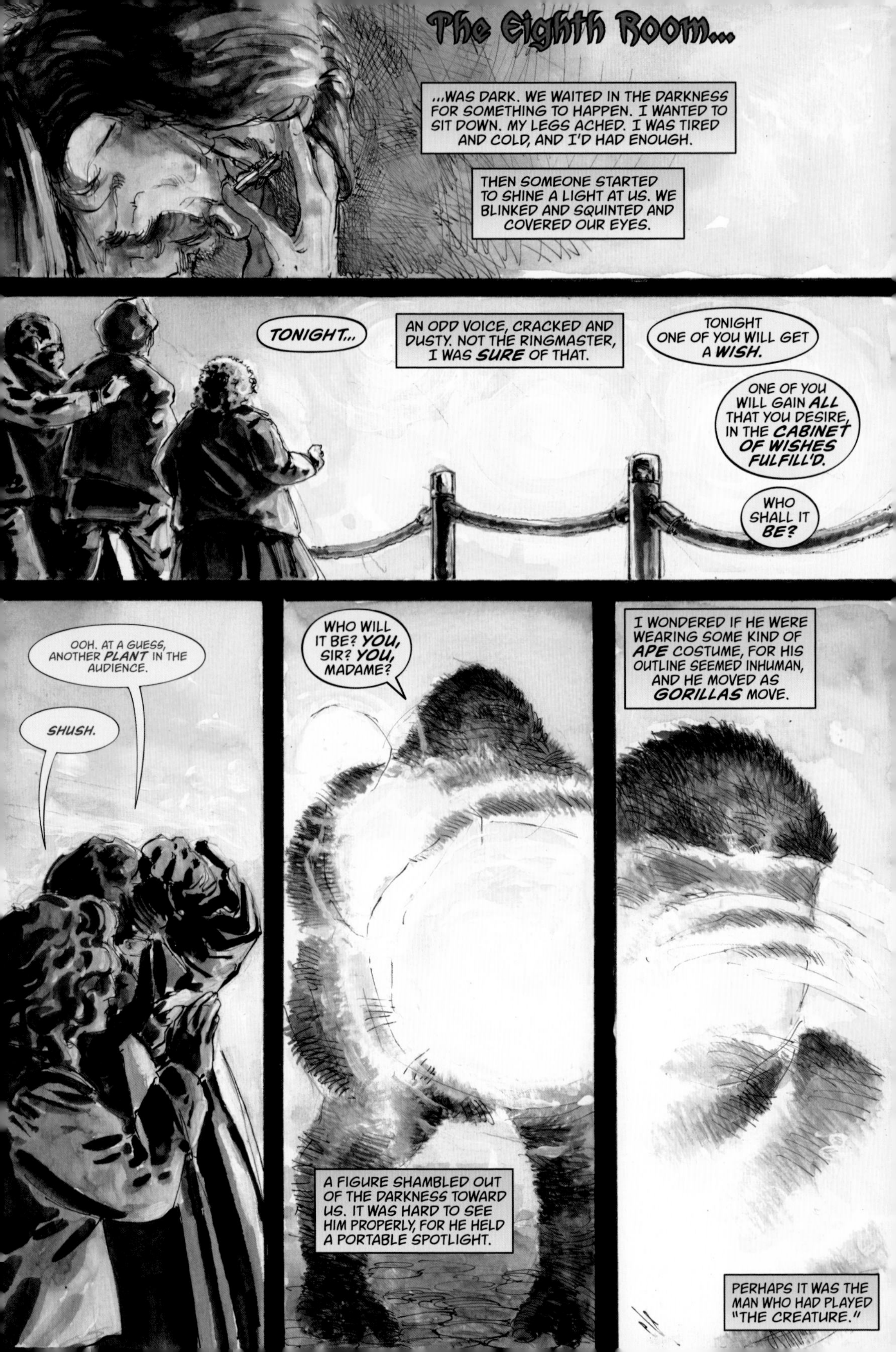
The Eighth Room...
...WAS DARK. WE WAITED IN THE DARKNESS FOR SOMETHING TO HAPPEN. I WANTED TO SIT DOWN. MY LEGS ACHED. I WAS TIRED AND COLD, AND I'D HAD ENOUGH.
THEN SOMEONE STARTED TO SHINE A LIGHT AT US. WE BLINKED AND SQUINTED AND COVERED OUR EYES.
TONIGHT...
AN ODD VOICE, CRACKED AND DUSTY. NOT THE RINGMASTER, I WAS SURE OF THAT.
TONIGHT ONE OF YOU WILL GET A WISH.
ONE OF YOU WILL GAIN ALL THAT YOU DESIRE, IN THE CABINET OF WISHES FULFILL'D.
WHO SHALL IT BE?
OOH. AT A GUESS, ANOTHER PLANT IN THE AUDIENCE.
SHUSH.
WHO WILL IT BE? YOU, SIR? YOU, MADAME?
A FIGURE SHAMBLED OUT OF THE DARKNESS TOWARD US. IT WAS HARD TO SEE HIM PROPERLY, FOR HE HELD A PORTABLE SPOTLIGHT.
I WONDERED IF HE WERE WEARING SOME KIND OF APE COSTUME, FOR HIS OUTLINE SEEMED INHUMAN, AND HE MOVED AS GORILLAS MOVE.
PERHAPS IT WAS THE MAN WHO HAD PLAYED "THE CREATURE."

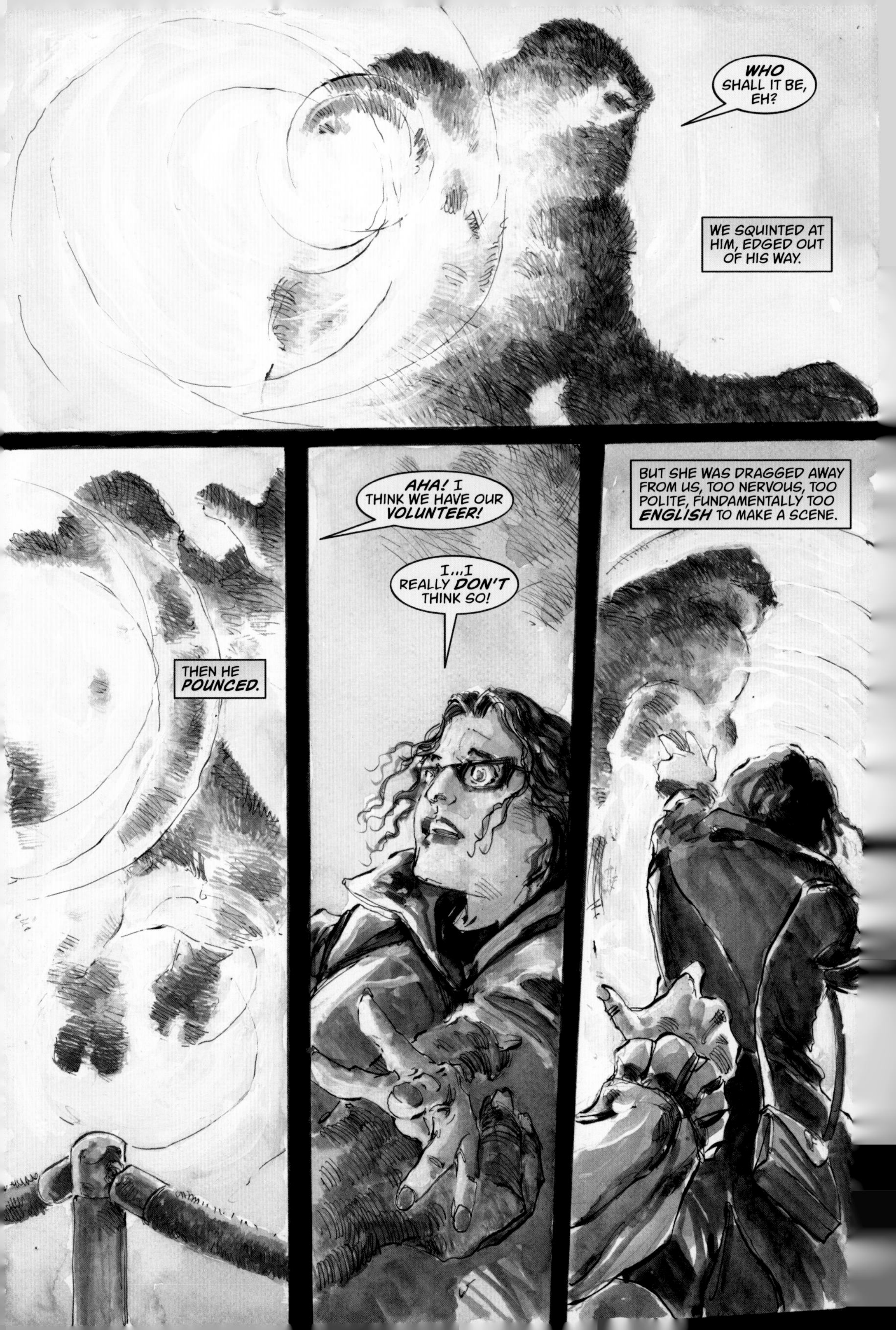
WHO SHALL IT BE, EH?
WE SQUINTED AT HIM, EDGED OUT OF HIS WAY.
THEN HE POUNCED.
AHA! I THINK WE HAVE OUR VOLUNTEER!
I...I REALLY DON'T THINK SO!
BUT SHE WAS DRAGGED AWAY FROM US, TOO NERVOUS, TOO POLITE, FUNDAMENTALLY TOO ENGLISH TO MAKE A SCENE.

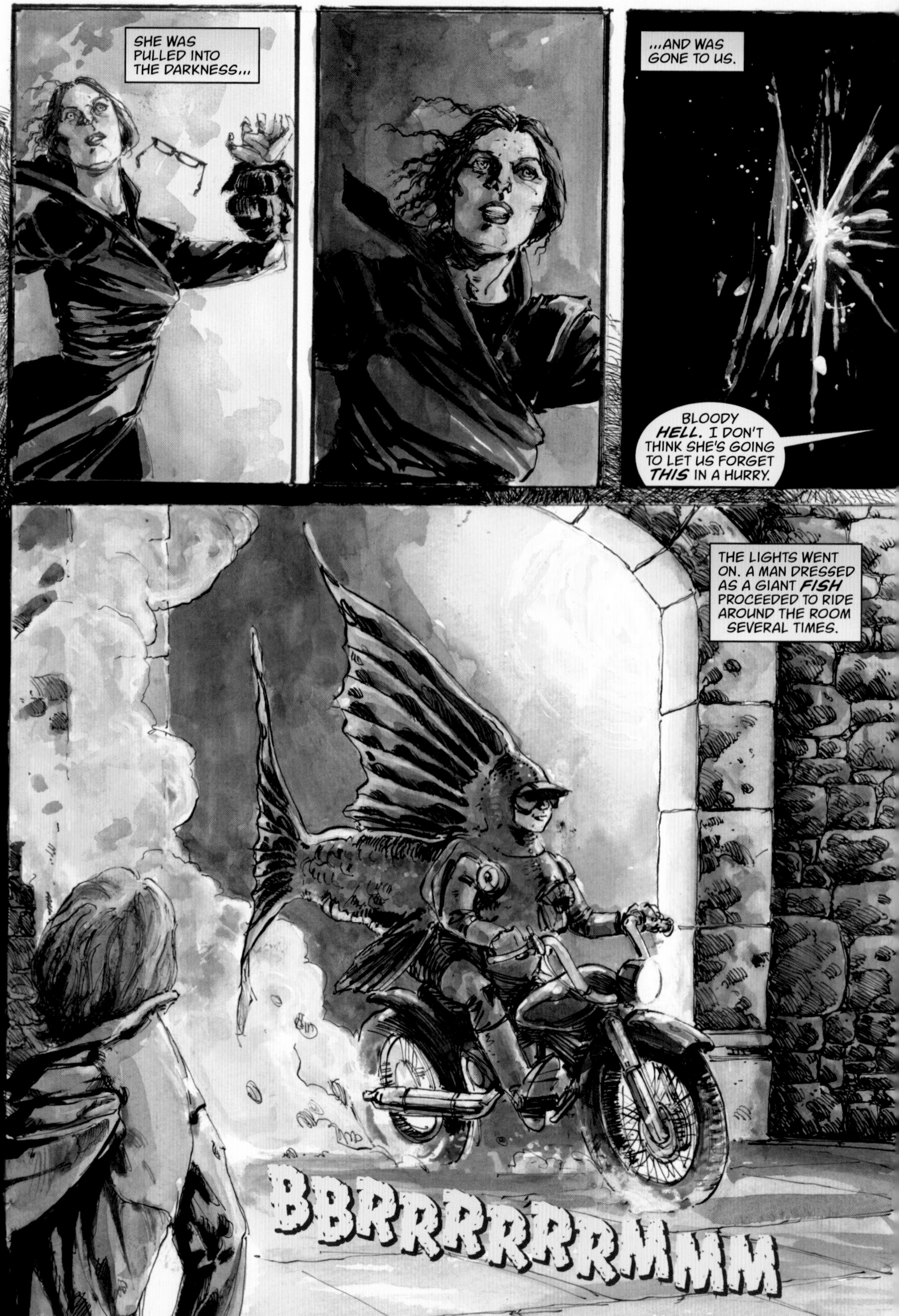
SHE WAS PULLED INTO THE DARKNESS...
...AND WAS GONE TO US.
BLOODY HELL. I DON'T THINK SHE'S GOING TO LET US FORGET THIS IN A HURRY.
THE LIGHTS WENT ON. A MAN DRESSED AS A GIANT FISH PROCEEDED TO RIDE AROUND THE ROOM SEVERAL TIMES.
BBRRRRRRRMMMM

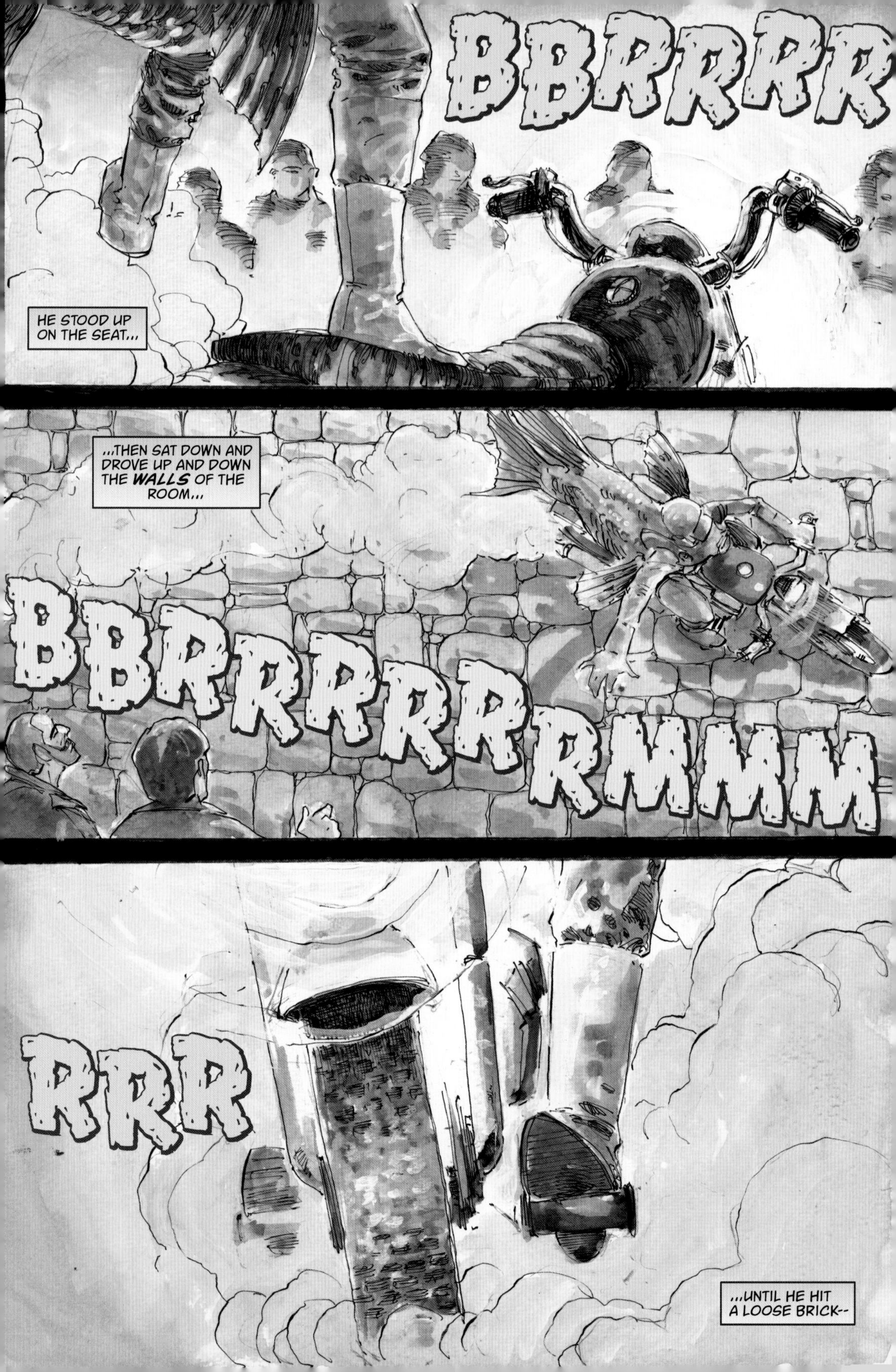
BBRRRR
HE STOOD UP ON THE SEAT...
...THEN SAT DOWN AND DROVE UP AND DOWN THE *WALLS* OF THE ROOM...
BBRRRRRRMMM
RRR
...UNTIL HE HIT A LOOSE BRICK--

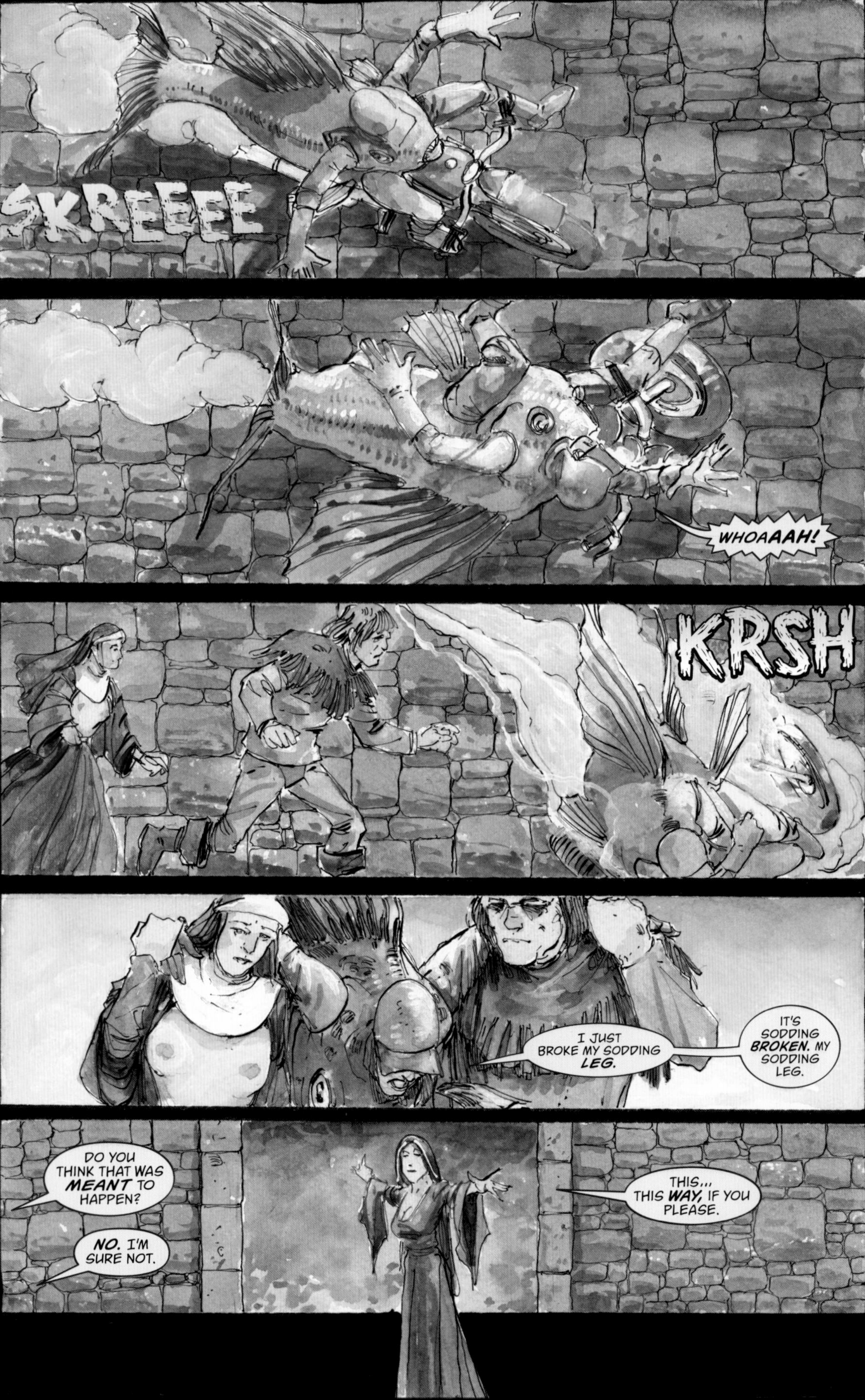
SKREEEE
WHOAAAH!
KRSH
I JUST BROKE MY SODDING LEG.
IT'S SODDING BROKEN. MY SODDING LEG.
DO YOU THINK THAT WAS MEANT TO HAPPEN?
NO. I'M SURE NOT.
THIS... THIS WAY, IF YOU PLEASE.

The Ninth Room

IT WAS A *HUGE* ROOM. I KNEW THAT, EVEN IN THE DIM MIST. PERHAPS THE DARK INTENSIFIES THE OTHER SENSES; PERHAPS IT'S SIMPLY THAT WE ARE ALWAYS PROCESSING MORE INFOR-MATION THAN WE IMAGINE.

ECHOES OF OUR COUGHING CAME BACK TO US FROM WALLS *HUNDREDS* OF FEET AWAY THROUGH WHAT SEEMED TO BE PRIMEVAL FOREST.

AND THEN I BECAME CONVINCED, WITH A CERTAINTY BORDERING ON MADNESS, THAT THERE WERE GREAT *BEASTS* IN THE ROOM...

...AND THAT THEY WERE WATCHING US *HUNGRILY*.

SLOWLY THE MIST CLEARED, AND WE SAW MISS FINCH.

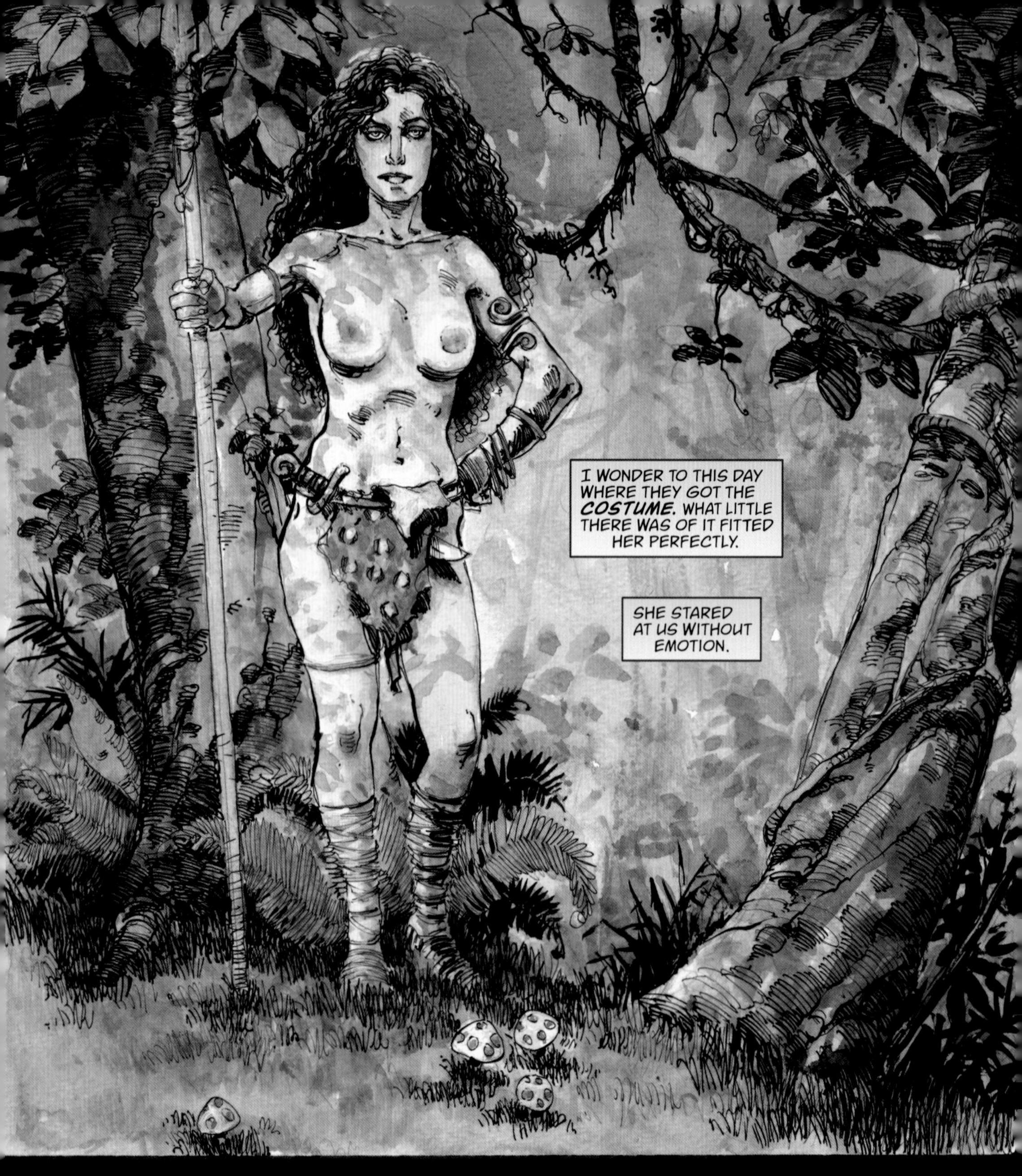
I WONDER TO THIS DAY WHERE THEY GOT THE COSTUME. WHAT LITTLE THERE WAS OF IT FITTED HER PERFECTLY.
SHE STARED AT US WITHOUT EMOTION.

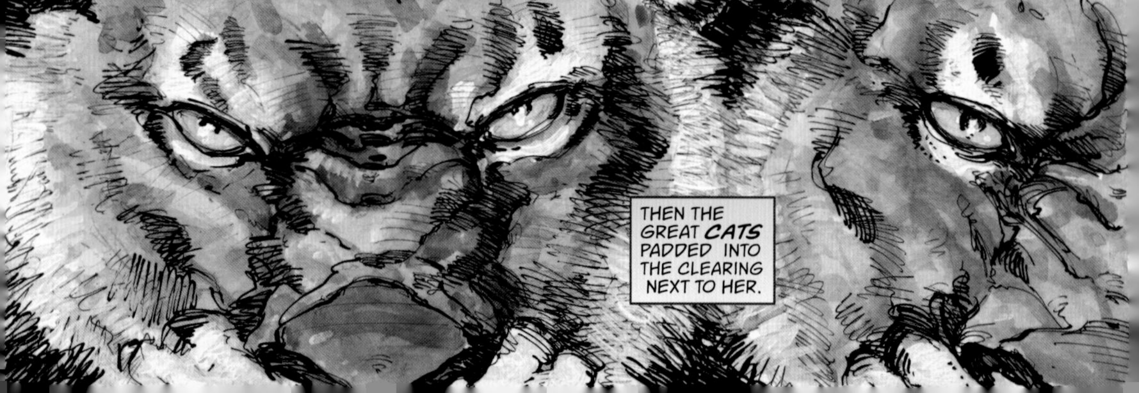
THEN THE GREAT CATS PADDED INTO THE CLEARING NEXT TO HER.

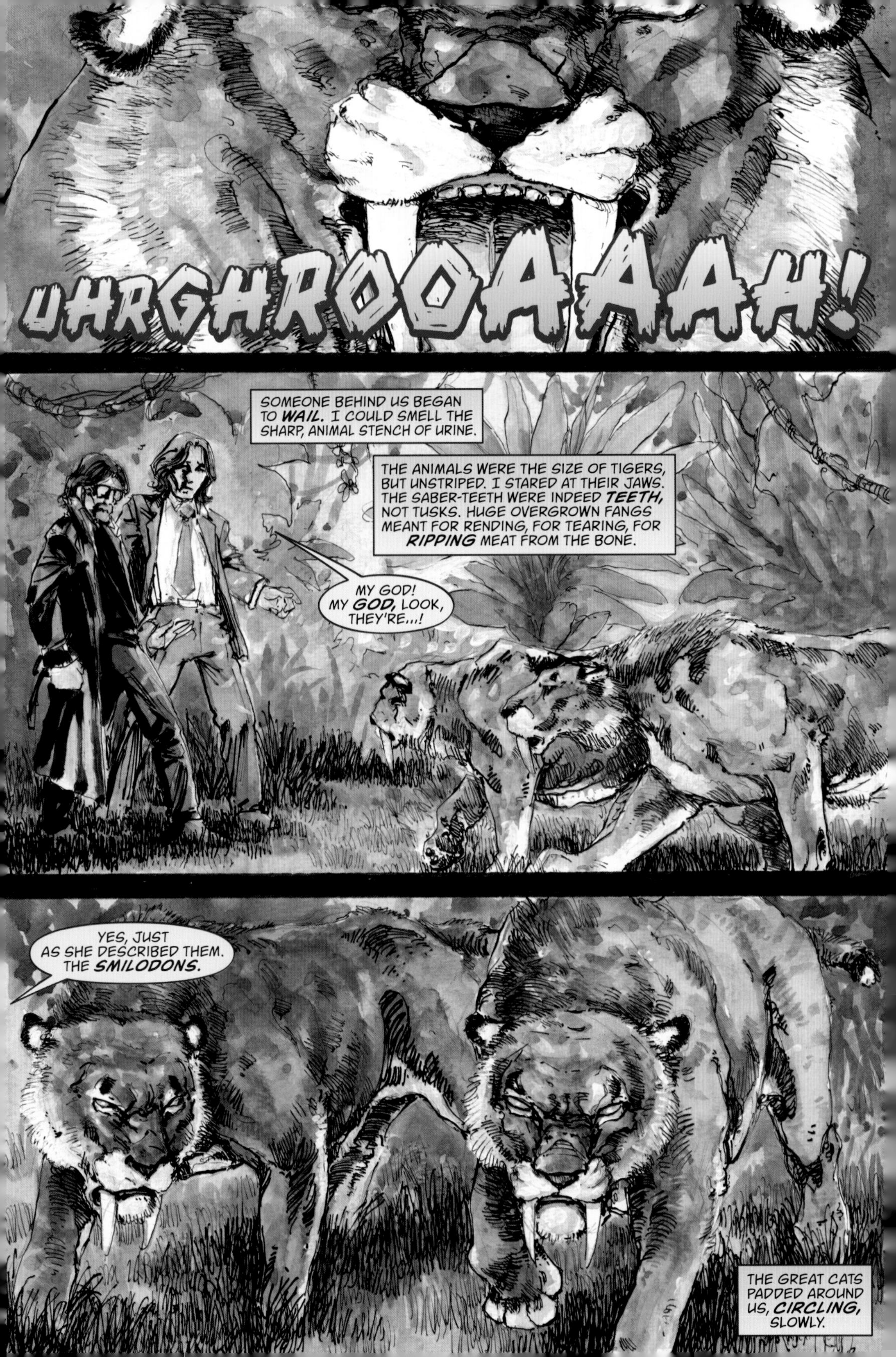
UHRGHROOAAAH!
SOMEONE BEHIND US BEGAN TO WAIL. I COULD SMELL THE SHARP, ANIMAL STENCH OF URINE.
THE ANIMALS WERE THE SIZE OF TIGERS, BUT UNSTRIPED. I STARED AT THEIR JAWS. THE SABER-TEETH WERE INDEED TEETH, NOT TUSKS. HUGE OVERGROWN FANGS MEANT FOR RENDING, FOR TEARING, FOR RIPPING MEAT FROM THE BONE.
MY GOD! MY GOD, LOOK, THEY'RE...!
YES, JUST AS SHE DESCRIBED THEM. THE SMILODONS.
THE GREAT CATS PADDED AROUND US, CIRCLING, SLOWLY.

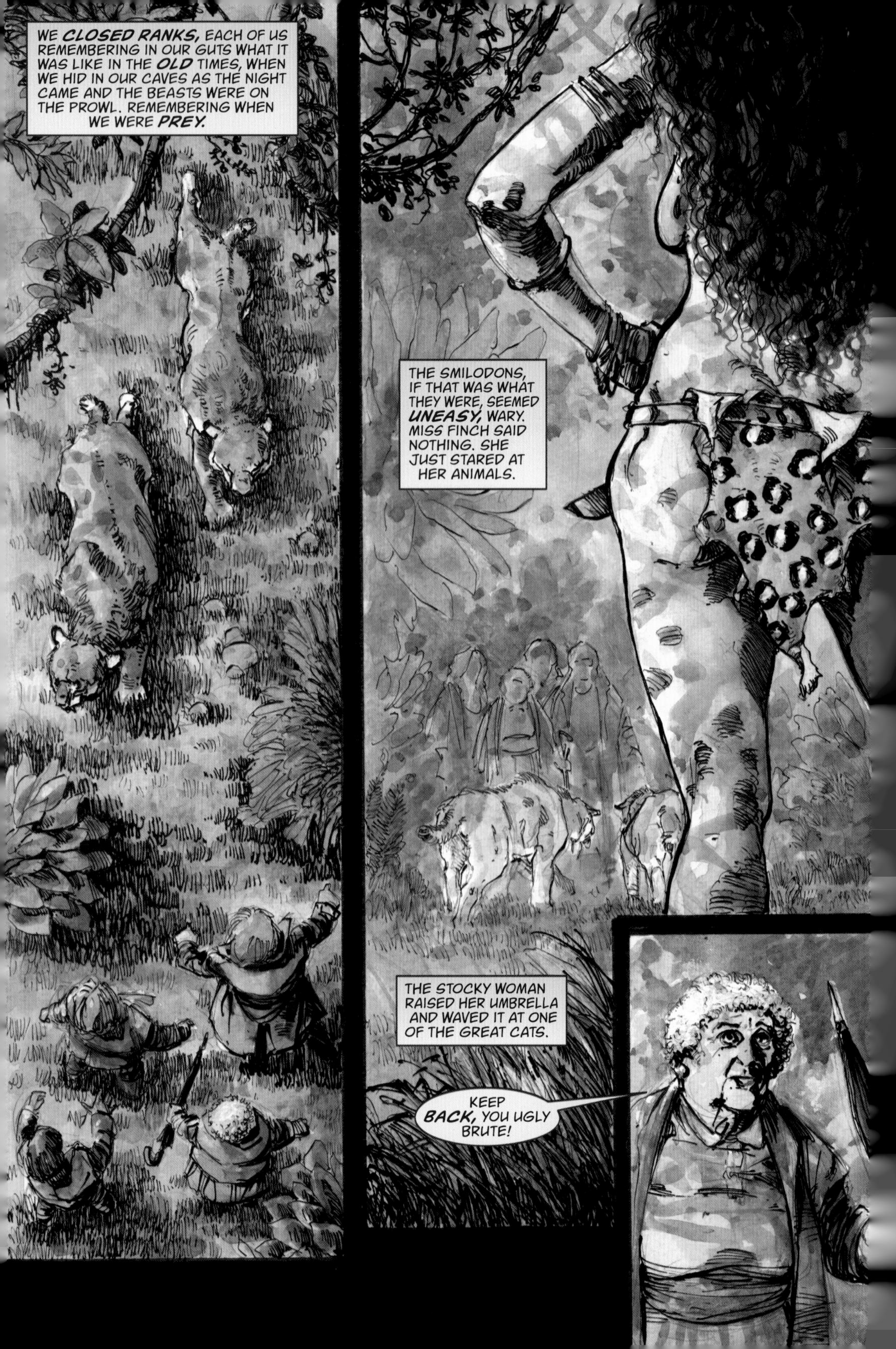
WE CLOSED RANKS, EACH OF US REMEMBERING IN OUR GUTS WHAT IT WAS LIKE IN THE OLD TIMES, WHEN WE HID IN OUR CAVES AS THE NIGHT CAME AND THE BEASTS WERE ON THE PROWL. REMEMBERING WHEN WE WERE PREY.
THE SMILODONS, IF THAT WAS WHAT THEY WERE, SEEMED UNEASY, WARY. MISS FINCH SAID NOTHING. SHE JUST STARED AT HER ANIMALS.
THE STOCKY WOMAN RAISED HER UMBRELLA AND WAVED IT AT ONE OF THE GREAT CATS.
KEEP BACK, YOU UGLY BRUTE!

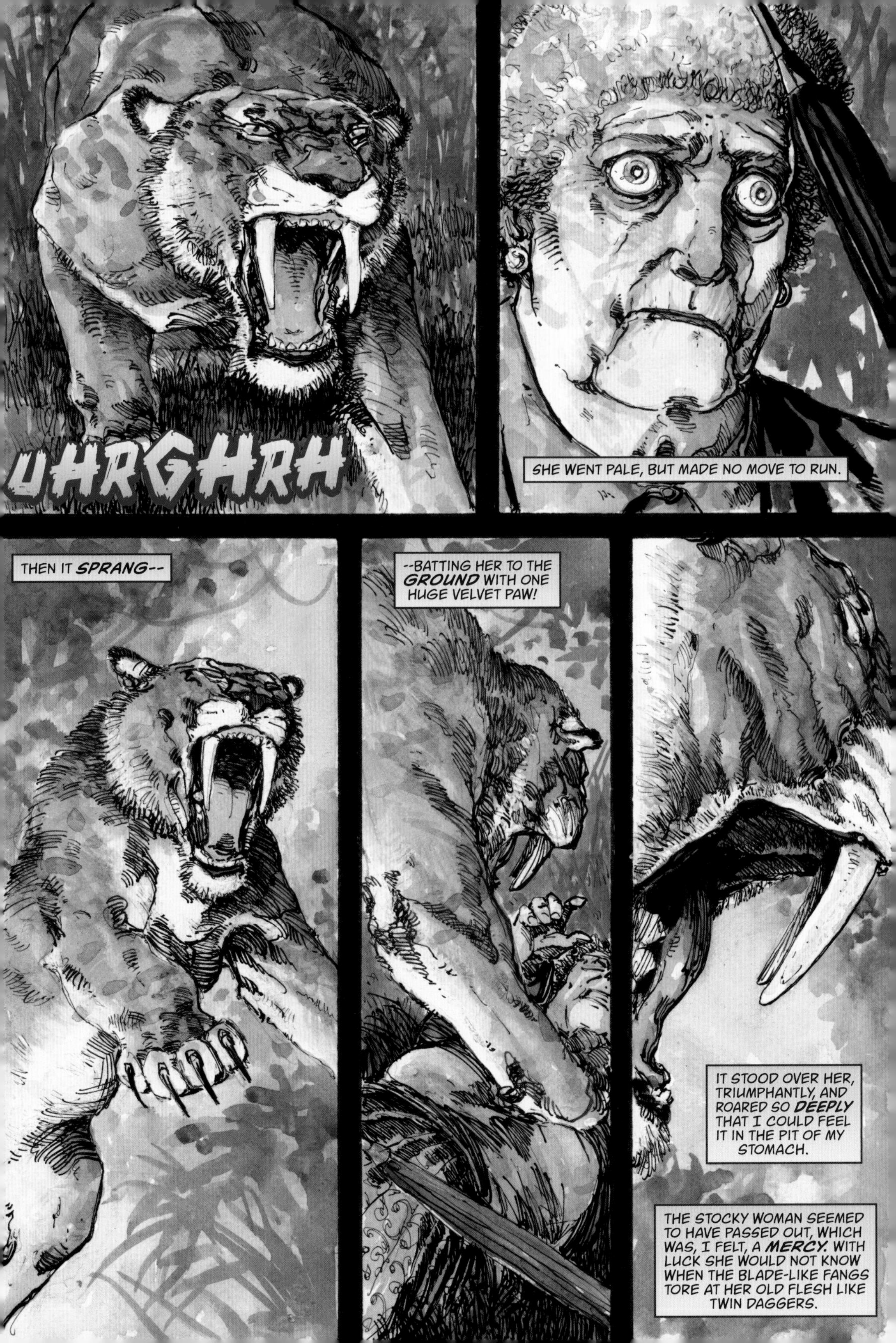
UHRGHRH
SHE WENT PALE, BUT MADE NO MOVE TO RUN.
THEN IT SPRANG--
--BATTING HER TO THE GROUND WITH ONE HUGE VELVET PAW!
IT STOOD OVER HER, TRIUMPHANTLY, AND ROARED SO DEEPLY THAT I COULD FEEL IT IN THE PIT OF MY STOMACH.
THE STOCKY WOMAN SEEMED TO HAVE PASSED OUT, WHICH WAS, I FELT, A MERCY. WITH LUCK SHE WOULD NOT KNOW WHEN THE BLADE-LIKE FANGS TORE AT HER OLD FLESH LIKE TWIN DAGGERS.

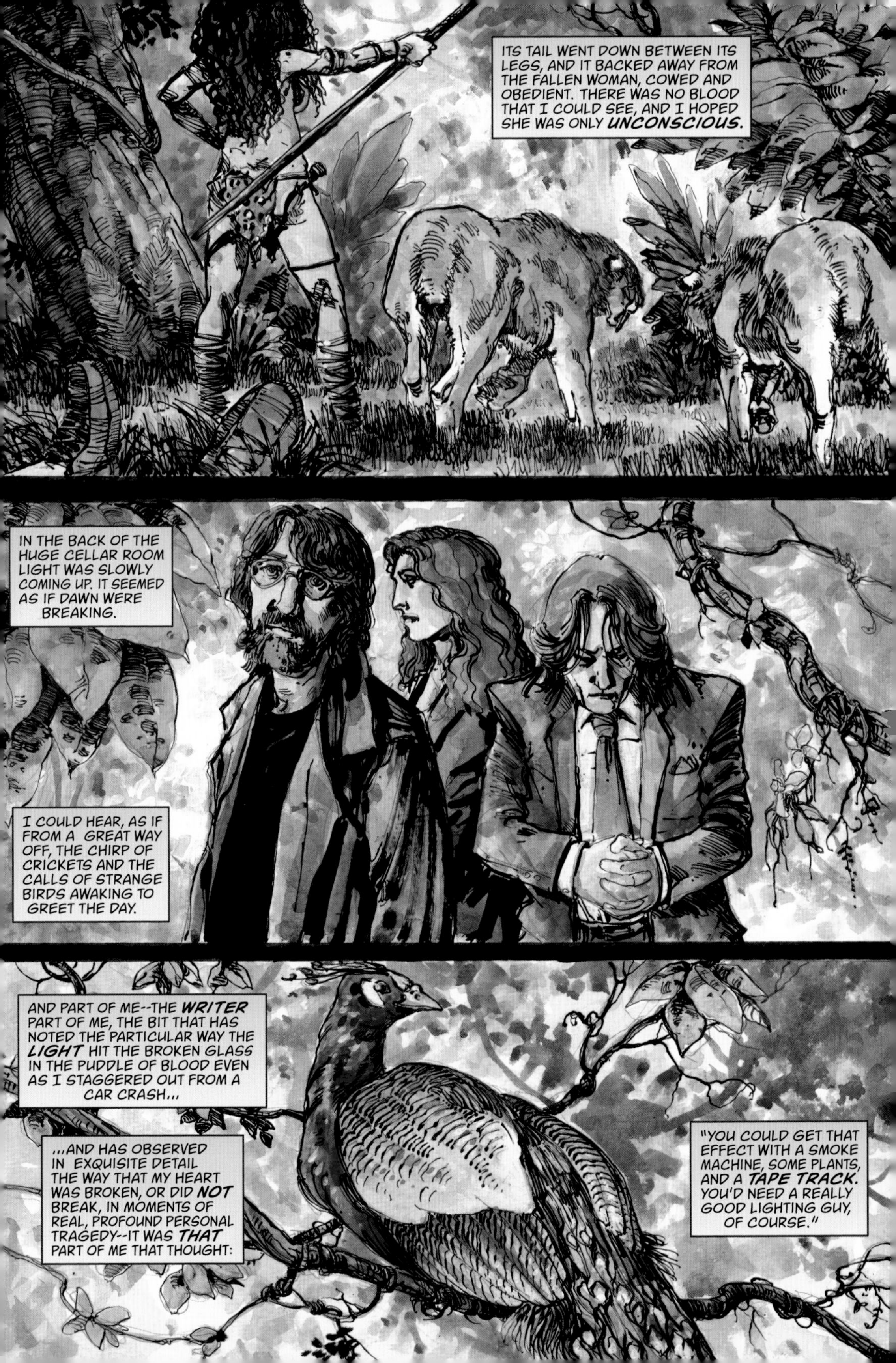
ITS TAIL WENT DOWN BETWEEN ITS LEGS, AND IT BACKED AWAY FROM THE FALLEN WOMAN, COWED AND OBEDIENT. THERE WAS NO BLOOD THAT I COULD SEE, AND I HOPED SHE WAS ONLY ***UNCONSCIOUS***.
IN THE BACK OF THE HUGE CELLAR ROOM LIGHT WAS SLOWLY COMING UP. IT SEEMED AS IF DAWN WERE BREAKING.
I COULD HEAR, AS IF FROM A GREAT WAY OFF, THE CHIRP OF CRICKETS AND THE CALLS OF STRANGE BIRDS AWAKING TO GREET THE DAY.
AND PART OF ME--THE ***WRITER*** PART OF ME, THE BIT THAT HAS NOTED THE PARTICULAR WAY THE ***LIGHT*** HIT THE BROKEN GLASS IN THE PUDDLE OF BLOOD EVEN AS I STAGGERED OUT FROM A CAR CRASH...
...AND HAS OBSERVED IN EXQUISITE DETAIL THE WAY THAT MY HEART WAS BROKEN, OR DID ***NOT*** BREAK, IN MOMENTS OF REAL, PROFOUND PERSONAL TRAGEDY--IT WAS ***THAT*** PART OF ME THAT THOUGHT:
"YOU COULD GET THAT EFFECT WITH A SMOKE MACHINE, SOME PLANTS, AND A ***TAPE TRACK***. YOU'D NEED A REALLY GOOD LIGHTING GUY, OF COURSE."

MISS FINCH GAVE US ONE LAST LONG, THOUGHTFUL LOOK, AS IF MAKING UP HER MIND...

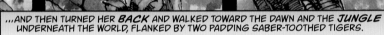

...AND THEN TURNED HER **BACK** AND WALKED TOWARD THE DAWN AND THE **JUNGLE** UNDERNEATH THE WORLD, FLANKED BY TWO PADDING SABER-TOOTHED TIGERS.

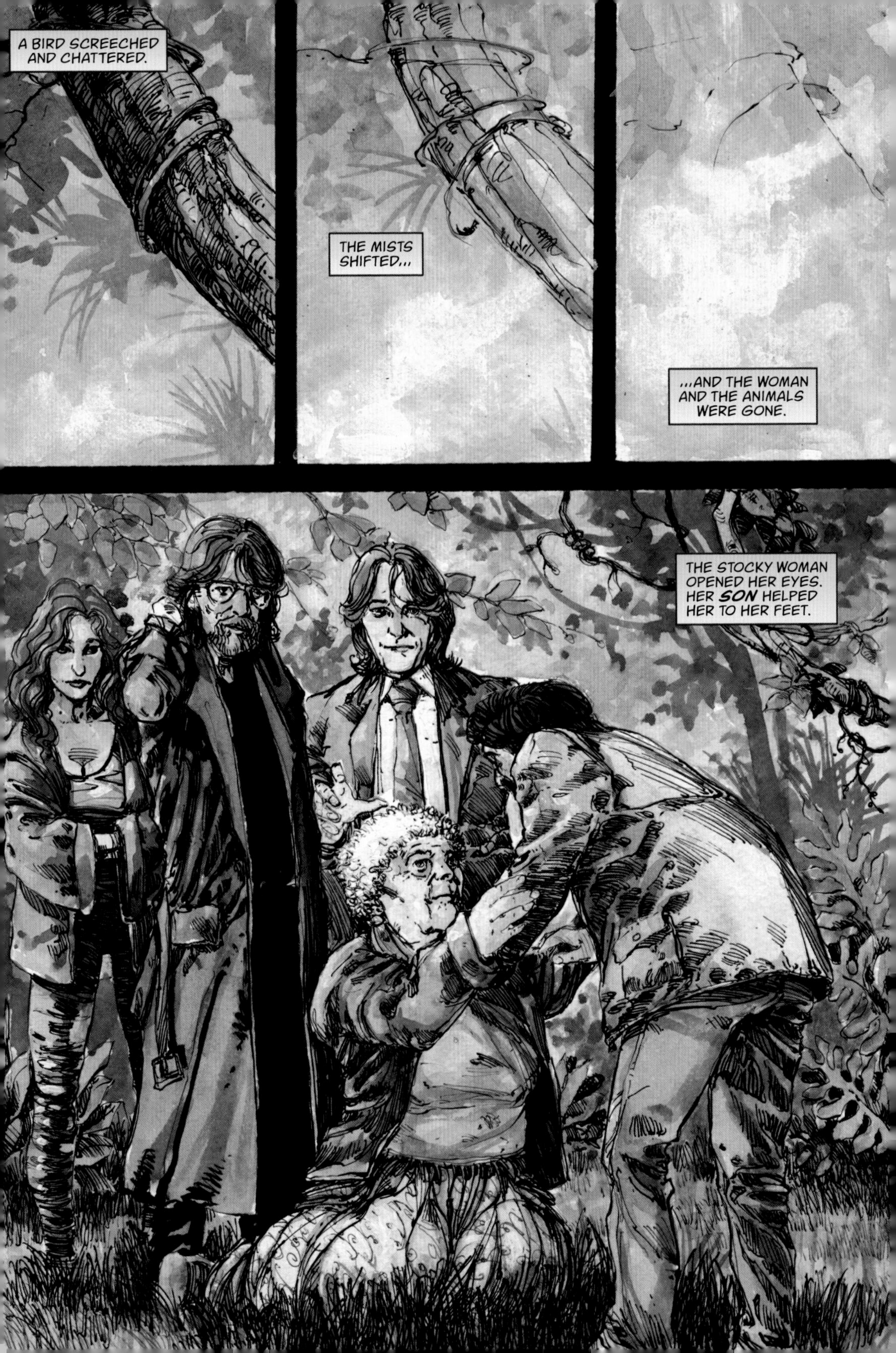
A BIRD SCREECHED AND CHATTERED.
THE MISTS SHIFTED...
...AND THE WOMAN AND THE ANIMALS WERE GONE.
THE STOCKY WOMAN OPENED HER EYES. HER SON HELPED HER TO HER FEET.

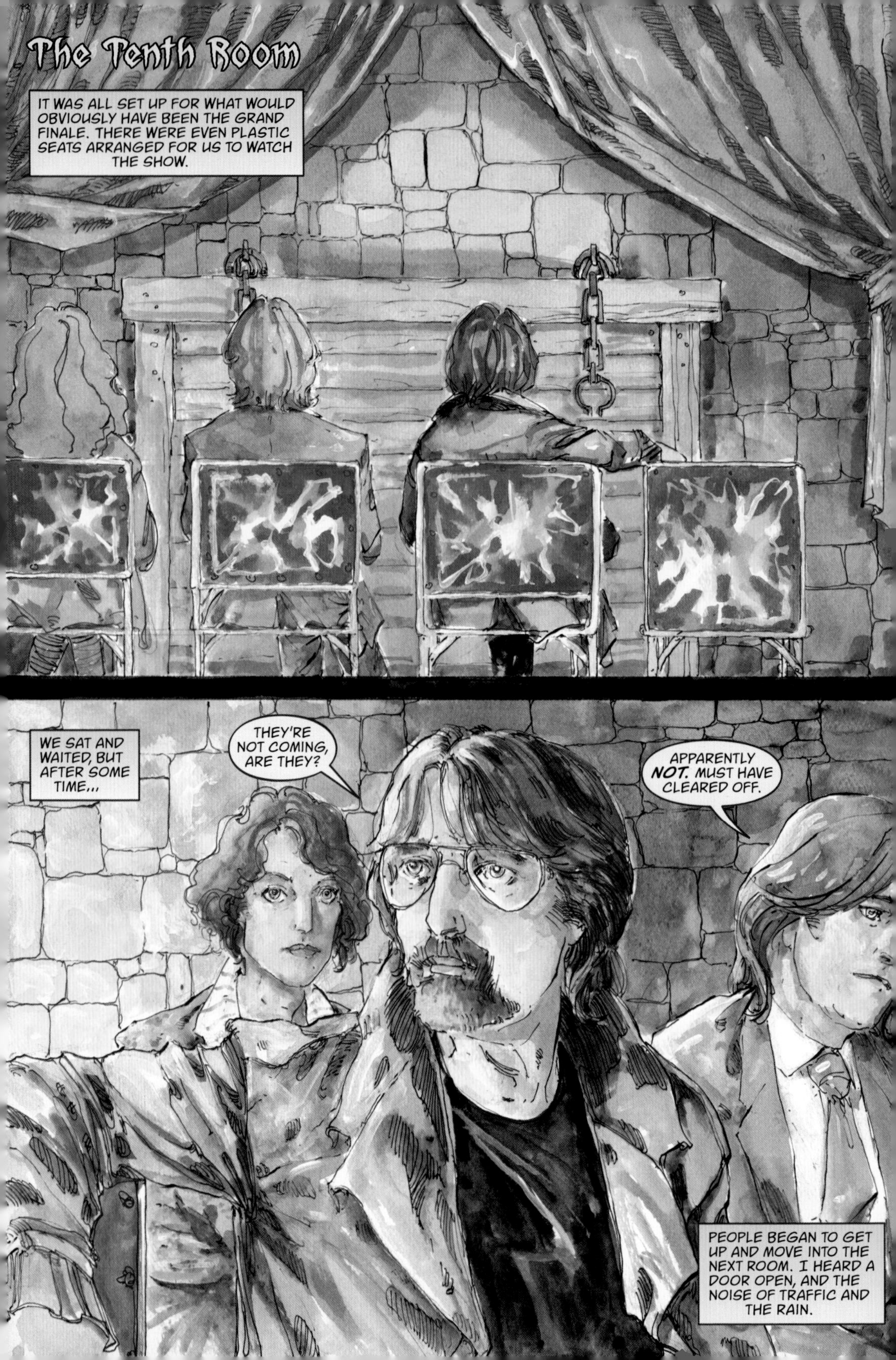
The Tenth Room
IT WAS ALL SET UP FOR WHAT WOULD OBVIOUSLY HAVE BEEN THE GRAND FINALE. THERE WERE EVEN PLASTIC SEATS ARRANGED FOR US TO WATCH THE SHOW.
WE SAT AND WAITED, BUT AFTER SOME TIME...
THEY'RE NOT COMING, ARE THEY?
APPARENTLY **NOT.** MUST HAVE CLEARED OFF.
PEOPLE BEGAN TO GET UP AND MOVE INTO THE NEXT ROOM. I HEARD A DOOR OPEN, AND THE NOISE OF TRAFFIC AND THE RAIN.

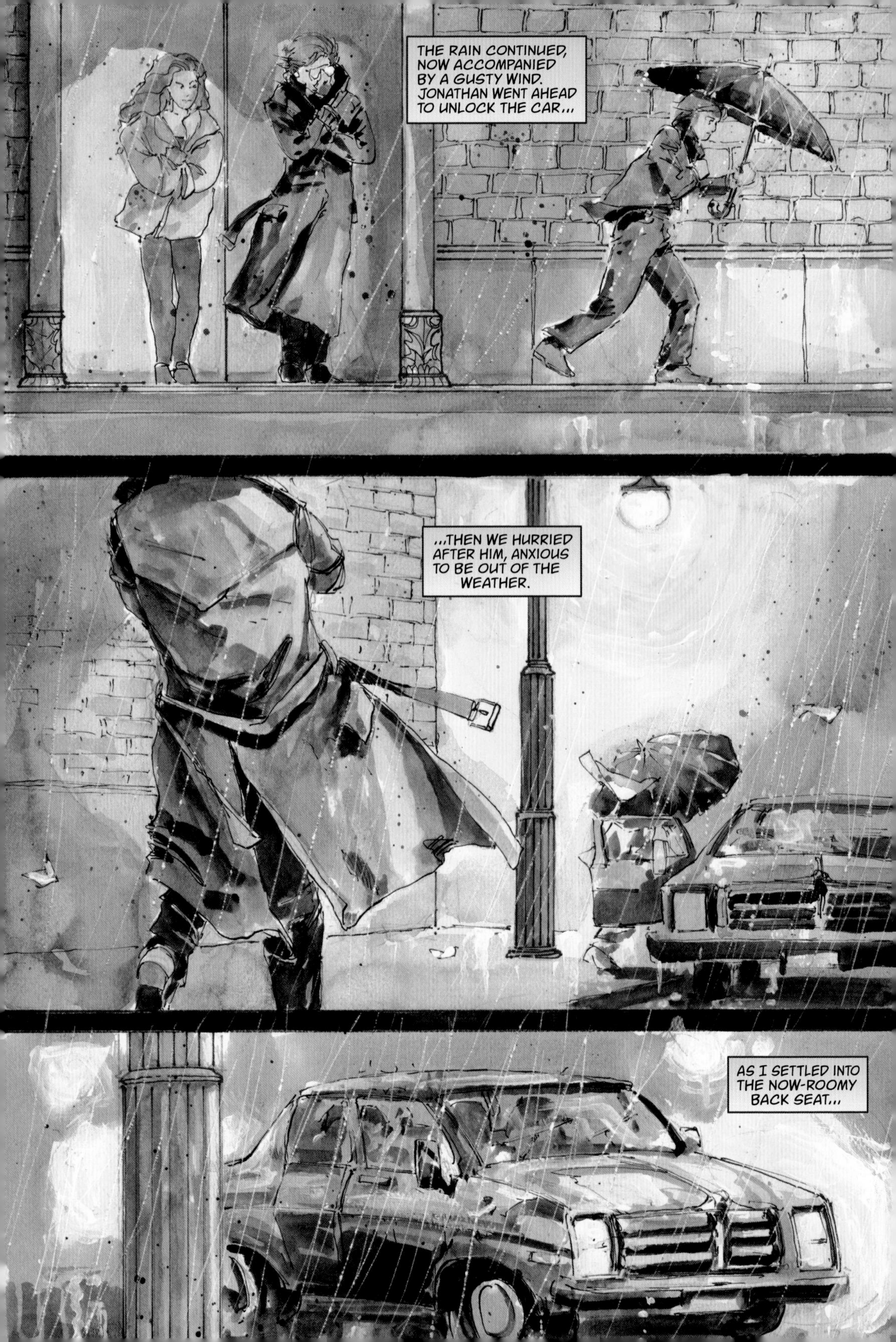
THE RAIN CONTINUED, NOW ACCOMPANIED BY A GUSTY WIND. JONATHAN WENT AHEAD TO UNLOCK THE CAR...
...THEN WE HURRIED AFTER HIM, ANXIOUS TO BE OUT OF THE WEATHER.
AS I SETTLED INTO THE NOW-ROOMY BACK SEAT...

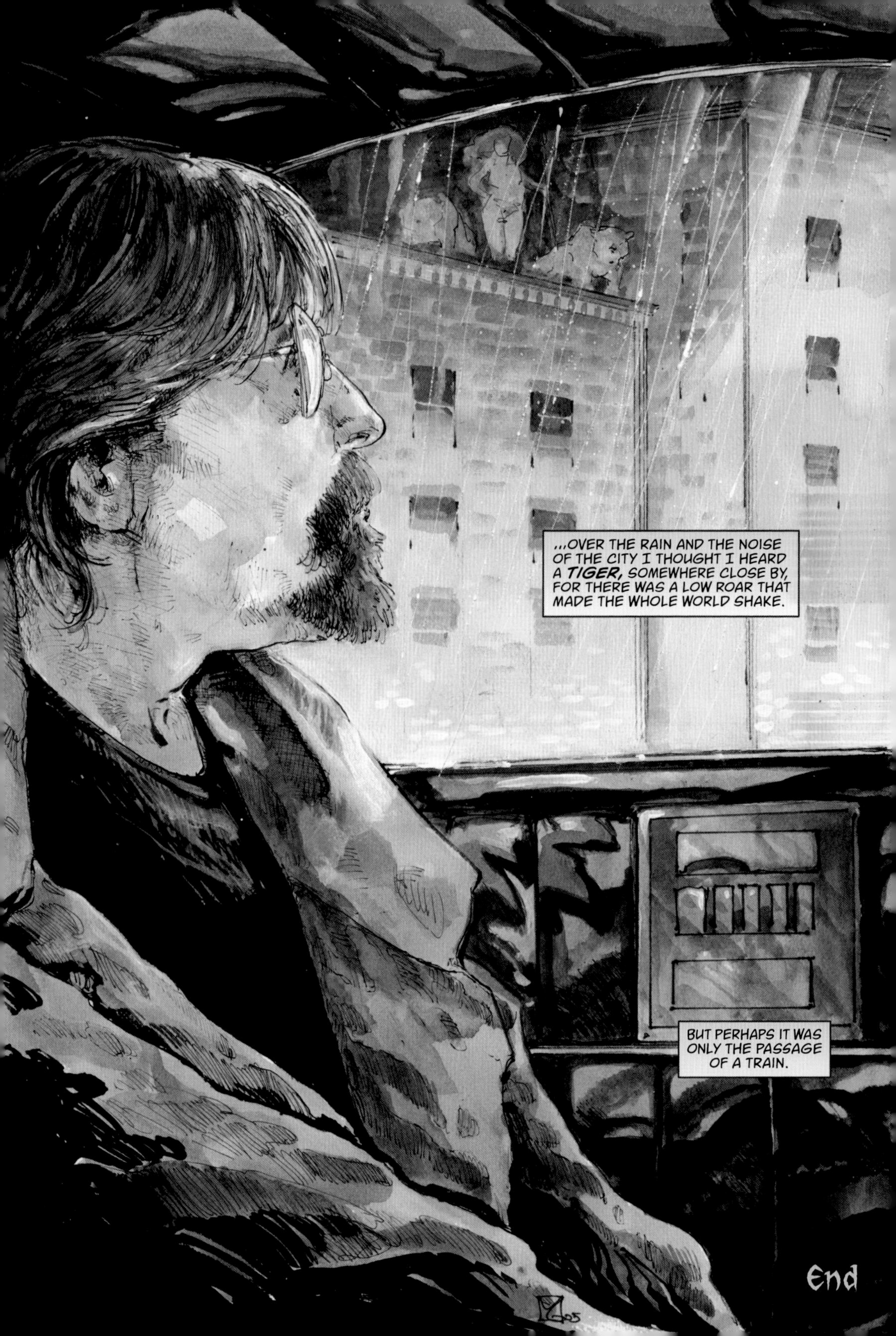
...OVER THE RAIN AND THE NOISE OF THE CITY I THOUGHT I HEARD A TIGER, SOMEWHERE CLOSE BY, FOR THERE WAS A LOW ROAR THAT MADE THE WHOLE WORLD SHAKE.
BUT PERHAPS IT WAS ONLY THE PASSAGE OF A TRAIN.
End

Photo by Sophia Quach

Gaiman is one of the most highly regarded writers of the m
prolific creator of prose, poetry, film, journalism, comics, song lyrics
began his best-known work in comics, the best-selling and aw
es *The Sandman*. Before that, he collaborated with artist Dave Mc
els, *Violent Cases* and *Signal to Noise*, both currently available from
s with McKean include the comics *Black Orchid* and *The Tragic*
gedy of *Mr. Punch*, the illustrated children's books *The Day I Swap*
dfish and *The Wolves in the Walls*, and the film *MirrorMask*, wh
McKean directed. As a novelist, Gaiman has penned many *Neu*
including *American Gods*, *Coraline*, *Anansi Boys*, and *The Gra*
both the Newbery Medal and the Carnegie Medal. In 2007, his n
into a major motion picture, and his script for *Beowulf*, cowritten
filmed by director Robert Zemeckis. Collections of his short p
Mirrors and *Fragile Things*, and his other comics work includes
2 for Marvel; *The Books of Magic, Death: The High Cost of Living*
Your Life for Vertigo; and *Harlequin Valentine*, *Murder Mysteries*, a

Michael Zulli begextra began his comics career in 1986 as the artist of *The Puma Blues*, written by Stephen Murphy. Published first by Aardvark-Vanaheim and later by Mirage Studios, the series ran for twenty-three issues and was renowned for its experimental storytelling techniques and message of environmental responsibility. Zulli also plotted, cowrote, and illustrated *Soul's Winter*, a *Teenage Mutant Ninja Turtles* trilogy for Mirage, now available in a collected edition. Zulli went on to illustrate a number of stories in Steve Bissette's horror anthology *Taboo*, and his profile skyrocketed after becoming one of the artists on Vertigo's best-selling and award-winning series *The Sandman*, written by Neil Gaiman. As frequent artistic collaborators, Zulli and Gaiman have completed several works together in addition to *The Sandman*, including *The Last Temptation*, a dark fable starring rock musician Alice Cooper, and *Creatures of the Night*, featuring two magical tales of humans and animals who are far from what they seem. Zulli was also the illustrator of J. Michael Straczynski's novella *Delicate Creatures*, published by Top Cow Productions. Zulli's latest work is a massive and deeply personal opus, *The Fracture of the Universal Boy*, published by Eidolon Fine Arts. He lives in Minnesota.

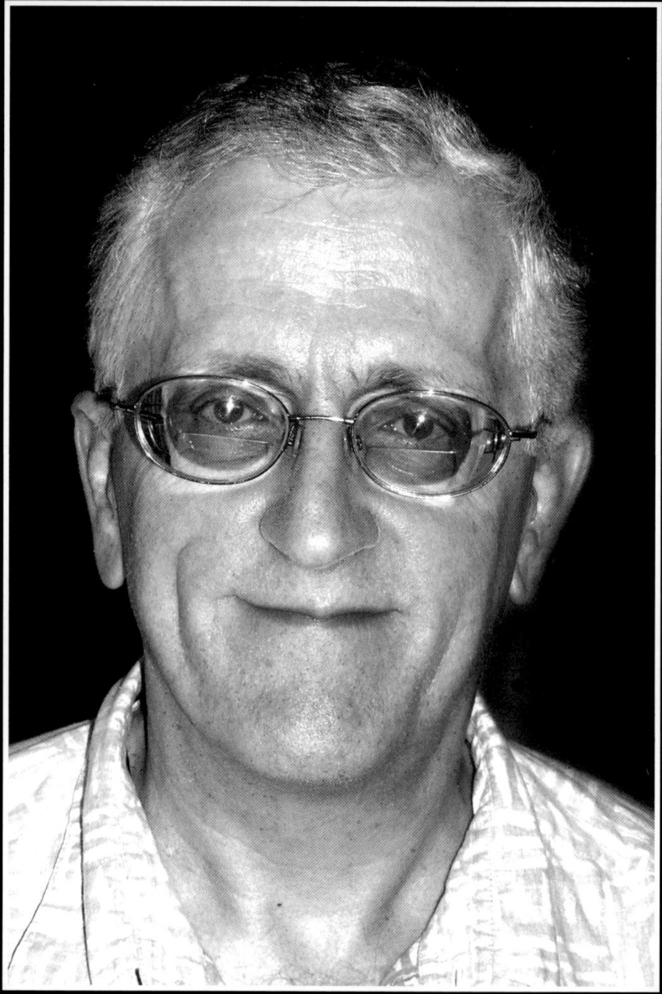

Photo by José Villarrubia

Todd Klein has established himself as one of the preeminent letterers of contemporary comics over the course of his nearly forty-year career. Beginning in the production department at DC Comics in 1977, he meticulously studied the work of letterers such as John Workman, John Costanza, and Gaspar Saladino, and was soon lettering and designing logos for many titles. During this time, Klein also wrote comics, including stories for *House of Mystery*, *Green Lantern*, and *The Omega Men*. In 1987, he became a full-time freelance letterer, shortly thereafter launching a long-running collaboration with writer Neil Gaiman on *The Sandman* from Vertigo. In addition to Gaiman, Klein worked with writer Alan Moore for over a decade on numerous projects, including lettering and designing for the America's Best Comics line at Wildstorm. He also authored the lettering section in *The DC Comics Guide to Coloring and Lettering Comics*. Klein's mastery has been recognized around the world, most notably with sixteen Eisner Awards and nine Harvey Awards. He continues to work avidly from his home in New Jersey, where he lives with his wife Ellen.